BRAKE Repair

HOW TO DIAGNOSE, FIX, OR REPLACE YOUR CAR'S BRAKES **STEP BY STEP**

Steven Cartwright

S·A DESIGN

CarTech®

CarTech®

CarTech®, Inc.
838 Lake Street South
Forest Lake, MN 55025
Phone: 651-277-1200 or 800-551-4754
Fax: 651-277-1203
www.cartechbooks.com

Edit by Bob Wilson
Layout by Hailey Samples

ISBN 978-1-61325-511-7
Item No. SA467

Library of Congress Cataloging-in-Publication Data

Names: Cartwright, Steven, 1955- author.
Title: Brake repair : how to diagnose, fix, or replace your car's brakes : step by step / Steven Cartwright.
Description: Forest Lake, MN : CarTech, Inc., 2020.
Identifiers: LCCN 2019037757 | ISBN 9781613255117 (paperback)
Subjects: LCSH: Automobiles--Brakes--Maintenance and repair--Handbooks, manuals, etc.
Classification: LCC TL269 .C37 2020 | DDC 629.2/460288--dc23
LC record available at https://lccn.loc.gov/2019037757

Written, edited, and designed in the U.S.A.
Printed in China
10 9 8 7 6 5 4 3 2 1

DISTRIBUTION BY:

Europe
PGUK
63 Hatton Garden
London EC1N 8LE, England
Phone: 020 7061 1980 • Fax: 020 7242 3725
www.pguk.co.uk

Australia
Renniks Publications Ltd.
3/37-39 Green Street
Banksmeadow, NSW 2109, Australia
Phone: 2 9695 7055 • Fax: 2 9695 7355
www.renniks.com

Canada
Login Canada
300 Saulteaux Crescent
Winnipeg, MB, R3J 3T2 Canada
Phone: 800 665 1148 • Fax: 800 665 0103
www.lb.ca

CONTENTS

ABOUT THE AUTHOR

Steven Cartwright resides in the country outside of St. Louis and has spent more than 40 years in the automotive field. He currently holds 30 ASE certifications.

After graduating from State Tech (Linn Tech) of Missouri in the 1970s, he worked as a technician and service manager for a nationwide auto chain. He moved on to become a line tech for a Ford dealer in St. Louis and then worked for Carter Carburetor and Tomco Carburetor in Los Angeles. He spent 27 years with Federal-Mogul as the curriculum development manager and corporate technical trainer for Moog Chassis and Wagner Brake, traveling the US and Canada. Most recently, he was a regional trainer for TBC in Florida and now teaches at a large automotive college in the Midwest, where he specializes in chassis, brake, driveline, and HVAC.

He earned the Top Tech Trainer of the Year award early in his career and has been involved with NACAT since 1985. He spent many years on college advisory boards and assists with ASE question writing workshops.

He and his wife, Terry, have been married almost 40 years and have a son, daughter-in-law, and grandson in Florida. Steven enjoys boats, muscle cars, touring and off-road motorcycles and has owned many over the years. With his son, he built a 1970 Chevelle that is still in the family, and he owns a 1952 Ford F2 flathead with his wife. He currently has 8 motorcycles. The family has a Dodge dually and a fifth-wheel toy hauler and enjoys camping with its motorcycles.

ACKNOWLEDGMENTS

Thank you to those who provided support before and during the production of this book in the form of education, emotional support, writing skills, photos, friendship, and understanding.

First of all, thank you to my wife, Terry, who let me put aside all of my honey-do lists and to the rest of my family and friends who didn't see a lot of me during the process. Mom, I will get to your lawn soon! Thanks for teaching me life skills and about the love of God.

To my son, Rob, who shares the love of all things automotive with me. I miss all those car shows we frequented when you were young, but I am glad we had the opportunity to build your 1970 Chevelle together when you were a teenager. You always shine with creativity.

To all the NACAT members and the folks at ASE who have supported me at the conventions and workshops.

To Jim Halderman, another author and teacher who I have been friends with for many decades, who I hold with the greatest respect for his unselfish help to me and the entire automotive industry. He will probably never actually retire because he cares too much. Many thanks for supplying some of the photos in this book. You're the absolute best, Jim!

To Clarence Vollmer who was my *Mr. Miyagi* at the Ford dealership back in the 1970s when I was an apprentice mechanic. Being on flat rate means that helping others can hurt your paycheck. Mr. Vollmer gave of himself and mentored me through those early days. He showed me the ropes in a way that improved my abilities and gave me confidence.

To Tye Hughes, who took me under his wing when I was starting out in this business and told me I could do it when I was asked to teach a class at Carter Carburetor unexpectedly. He believed in me and pushed me to become an automotive instructor against my wishes, which has been a very rewarding experience for the last 35-plus years.

To Roger Creason, a great friend and teacher and the best man in the alignment business. Thanks for helping me both technically and to become a better educator.

To my good friend Mark Baker, who built a go-cart with me when we were kids and became my boss years later at Federal-Mogul. Also to all those in Mark's department who helped me: you know who you are. Thanks, guys and gals.

To Randy Wright, Mark Riecks, Dan Smith, Mark Isaac, and others who helped me develop a love of everything mechanical from all the stuff we tore apart over the years and sometimes put back together.

You all deserve a lot more than my thanks because you gave of yourselves. This industry is a just a big family. Thanks for making me feel welcome. It has been quite a ride.

DEDICATION

To my dad, who was taken away from us much too early. He loved
all things mechanical and started me on this journey by taking the
time to help me fix my bike and tear a lawn mower engine apart.
I miss you every day.

INTRODUCTION

Congratulations on doing your own brake job! You have made the decision to learn a new skill or improve an existing one. Doing so will give you the satisfaction of completing an important, very critical task. At the completion, you will know it was done right and you will save some money too. You will also be able to assist your family and friends to help them save some money or maybe even earn some extra money. It is no secret that the brakes on your vehicle cannot be taken lightly and that the proper procedures are critical to your safety and others on the road. The proper procedures are also critical to your safety when working on your brakes. Please read and understand everything before you touch the first bolt or remove the first wheel cover.

This book is divided into 10 chapters. Although each chapter is specific to a particular subject related to brake systems and could be used on its own, you are encouraged to read the entire book before tackling a brake job. The book begins with an overview of brake systems and their history, which is followed by the components that comprise the system.

Following that, specifics about disc brakes, drum brakes, parking brakes, and the hydraulic system are provided. The hydraulic system supplies the force to apply the brakes at the wheels and must be carefully inspected, serviced, and bled during the brake job. Your vehicle uses a brake assist system to increase the force that you apply to the brake pedal. The next chapter covers how that is accomplished: with vacuum, power steering pressure, or electrically. All components, operation, diagnosis, and service steps are included in each of these chapters.

You will also find a chapter on troubleshooting, outlining common brake problems and their causes. Another chapter covers ABS and electronic brake systems. These systems interact with the base brake system you will be working on, so you need to know some details about their operation and precautions related to them. Also included is a glimpse into the future of how brake systems will evolve when ADAS and autonomous vehicles become more common on the road.

In addition to using this book, it is also very important to refer to the factory service information for specific details about the system you are working on. For example, some newer electronically controlled brake systems require that the system be put into service mode prior to repairs. The system has the ability to perform a self-test, which can pressurize the hydraulic system without warning. This could cause injury if the hydraulic system is open or your hands are in a component, such as a brake caliper, during service. Some models have electric parking brakes that may require a special procedure to retract the caliper so new brakes can be installed. In addition to the service manual that is normally available online, a technical service bulletin (TSB) may be available from the manufacturer to explain an update or common issue related to your vehicle.

After reading this book, you will have a good knowledge of automotive and light truck brake systems. With some common tools and a few special ones, brake work could become something you look forward to. The final chapter provides a step-by-step overview to performing a complete brake job on a disc and drum brake vehicle with photos explaining every step. It can be used as an outline after reading the detailed chapters that cover the specifics with greater depth.

Again, congratulations on learning a new skill!

BASIC BRAKE OPERATION

When you come to a stop sign, your vehicle has to be able to stop, and when it comes to safety, brakes are critically important.

Safety

Automobile manufacturers of the 1960s and 1970s boasted seat belts, safety glass, radial tuned suspension, safety cages, radial tires, and crumple zones. Since then, we've seen airbags, back-up cameras, and a long list of other safety-related updates. Antilock Brake Systems (ABS) have been around for more than 30 years, and now with the addition of Advanced Driver Assistance Systems (ADAS) and autonomous vehicles with no steering wheels on the horizon, we are moving into a new level of safety. The promise of these systems may completely eliminate vehicle fatalities someday.

Electronics have made this possible and are a big part of our lives and the modern vehicle, but there will always be a need for basic brake maintenance. The friction components are wear items and must be replaced at some point. Unless we jump to hovering vehicles on magnetism, air, or some other means, we will continue to have wheels that must be stopped.

You need to also consider your own safety when working on your vehicle's brake system. Safety glasses or a face shield, gloves, a dust mask, and ear protection (if rotary cleaning tools, impacts, or air hammers are used) are all important so that you are not injured while doing the work. Doing the job right is also extremely important to your safety and those around you, so be sure to read and fully understand the contents of this book before you begin.

I have tried to cover all the details, but because brake systems vary in design, you should consult your vehicle's service information or speak to a professional technician for specific procedures and specifications. Your local auto parts store can be a big help too.

Automotive brake systems are obviously important to vehicle safety and must be in excellent working condition, ready to perform in all conditions. Over the years, improvements have been made to greatly enhance driver assistance and comfort. Electronics have made it possible for engineers to blend the brake system into other vehicle systems, but the basic brake system has not changed all that much since its early designs.

Automotive Brake Systems

Believe it or not, the first vehicles had no brakes. Drum brakes were the first brake system used on early vehicles, but they did not use brake shoes like we know today.

History

The first designs used a flexible friction band that clamped around the outside of the drum that the wheel bolted to, like a band in an automatic transmission.

Most vehicles had them only on the rear axle. When the brake pedal was applied, a long metal rod from the brake pedal moved a lever that squeezed the band around the spinning drum, hopefully bringing it to a halt. No hydraulics were used at that time and this design was also subject to water contamination and rust since it was exposed to the elements. Needless to say, the system required a lot of pedal force to stop. You might think vehicles didn't go fast enough to require much force, but actually vehicles in that era could achieve highway speeds and were extremely heavy, so accidents

This 1919 Buick has a basic rear brake–only system that squeezes friction bands around spinning drums with mechanical rods to the brake pedal. Highway speeds were possible with this vehicle, which made braking an interesting experience.

were pretty common due to inadequate brakes.

Eventually, internal brake shoes replaced the external band on drum brake systems and they were added to all four wheels, but hydraulics were still not used. The systems remained mechanical. This made it difficult

for brake engineers because the front wheels must turn, and the mechanical linkages to the brakes must accommodate this. Enter hydraulics.

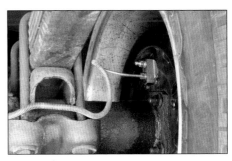

Hydraulics provide the same function as mechanical rods but are flexible and can route around obstructions and move with the suspension and steering systems. The term "hydraulic advantage" is used to explain how different-sized pistons can increase force inside of a brake system. If an input piston attached to the brake pedal is smaller than the output piston that applies the brake shoe or pad, the force is increased.

The external band (arrow) that applied around the drum was very similar to those used inside of an automatic transmission but were exposed to the elements. As a result, they were greatly affected by rain and dirt contamination. Rust was also a common problem with this design.

Mechanically applied drum brake systems used long metal rods between a lever at the brake pedal and levers at the rear axle (arrows). Because the axle moves up and down when the suspension moves, brake pulsations could occur when stopping.

When brake engineers added hydraulics to apply the shoes inside the drums, brake systems became extremely effective and reliable. Hydraulic fluid within a closed system acts like a solid metal rod, but it can be routed around components and pass through flexible hoses so that the front wheels can turn and the vehicle suspension can move freely. Hydraulic principles also allow for different piston diameters to be used between the master cylinder (input at the driver's foot) and the wheel cylinder (output to the brake shoes) so that pedal force and travel can be varied to best suit the driver and vehicle type.

Some of these early designs use a wheel cylinder with a single piston pushing on only one shoe. When the shoe touches the spinning drum, rotational forces cause energy to transfer to the other shoe and wedge it into the drum to stop the vehicle. This is known as self-energizing, or servo action.

Brake Adjustments

Today's rear drum brake systems look very similar to those on a 1957 Chevy, but early vehicles required routine brake adjustments to maintain pedal height as the brake shoes wore away. As a child, I recall seeing signs at nearly every gas station that read, "Brake adjustments while you wait: $3." ∎

In those early days, drum brakes were used on all four wheels and they really haven't changed much since then. Early drum brake systems did not automatically adjust, but modern vehicles with drum brakes have automatic adjuster systems that take care of this for you provided everything is assembled properly and not rusted or damaged.

Four-wheel drum power brakes with automatic adjusting capability became commonplace in the late 1960s and early 1970s. A vacuum-controlled booster was added between the brake pedal and the master cylinder that greatly increased the force, allowing virtually anyone to stop a heavy vehicle with minimal pedal effort. This system was a great improvement, but drum brakes are susceptible to water and use many moving parts that can develop problems. If water got in one front brake during a rainstorm or one side was not properly adjusting, the vehicle pulled to one side when stopping. Drum brakes also tend to retain heat and generate a lot of wear material that can get between the friction surfaces, reducing efficiency.

Then along came disc brakes. They were first used in aviation and have many advantages over drum brakes. They can shed dust and squeegee water off as soon as they are applied.

The typical drum brake system has remained virtually unchanged for many decades. A hydraulic wheel cylinder expands when the brakes are applied, which presses the brake shoes into the inside of the spinning brake drum to stop the vehicle.

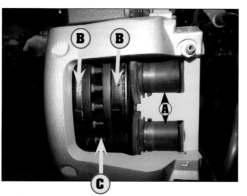

Some early drum brake systems used a wheel cylinder with only one piston, such as on this 1952 Ford F2 pickup truck. The piston (arrow) pushes the front shoe into the spinning drum. The spinning drum causes force to be applied to the other shoe, which wedges it into the drum and stops the vehicle. This concept is known as self-energizing or servo action. This truck has four-wheel drum brakes with no assist.

A conventional disc brake system uses a brake caliper over a spinning rotor. When the brakes are applied, piston(s) in the caliper (A) press brake pads (B) into the rotor (C) to stop the vehicle. Disc brakes are widely used on today's cars and light trucks because they are superior to drum brakes in almost every way.

They can dissipate heat well and automatically adjust to wear hydraulically, requiring no mechanical methods. They were first used on the front, and drums remained on the rear, but most of today's vehicles use disc brakes on all four wheels. They are extremely reliable and easier to service.

Electronics and Brake Systems

Antilock brakes were first used on trains and airplanes and became mainstream in the United States in the mid-1980s on the rear of many pickup trucks and vans. ABS provided a solution to the problem of rear wheel lockup when the vehicle was unloaded, which could lead to an accident, especially on a curve in the rain. As systems were improved and better sensors and data processing came about, ABS was added to all four wheels. The main goal of ABS is to allow a driver to steer around obstructions during a panic stop. It does this by keeping the wheels from totally locking, which would eliminate the ability to steer.

If you have ever ridden a personal watercraft and released the throttle while attempting to steer, you know what happens: You can't steer. ABS is also the basis for other safety systems on modern vehicles, such as stability control and traction control. Some applications use ABS for automatic stopping and during distance-based cruise control operation. This system will be even more important when autonomous vehicles become more common.

Many high-end and hybrid vehicles use electronic braking. Most of them do not use a traditional master cylinder to push the brake fluid to the wheels. A pedal travel sensor attached to the brake pedal monitors the driver's intentions and an electronic pressure modulator sends the fluid to the wheels. This sensor may be a chamber of brake fluid with transducers that convert pressure into electronic signals. The system can send different amounts of pressure to each wheel depending on varying driving conditions such as cornering or panic stopping. This allows for more effective control and a greater level of safety.

Some of these systems have had issues but most use some form of backup system in the event of system failure. Valves may open in the pressure transducers, allowing fluid to flow to the front calipers for

Some late-model, high-end, and hybrid vehicles use electronic brake systems. These systems generally use an electronic modulator to apply the brakes instead of a conventional master cylinder. This design allows for various pressures to be applied to each wheel relative to operating conditions.

An antilock braking system (ABS) uses a computer module to control pulsing action, improving steering and control during braking on slippery surfaces or during panic stopping situations. In many cases, stopping distance is also reduced because the brakes are applied to the point just before wheel lockup. The main advantage of ABS is being able to steer during an emergency stop.

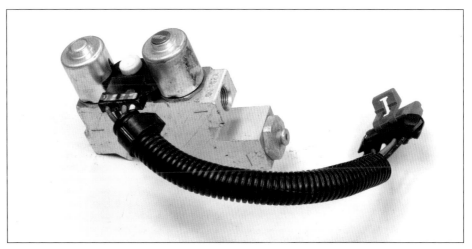

The mechanical unit that pulses the brakes during ABS operation is called the modulator. It contains two solenoids in series with the affected wheel. Early systems only controlled the rear wheels. One valve blocked the fluid and the other vented the high-pressure fluid to an accumulator, which released the rear brakes. The system was known as rear wheel antilock (RWAL) or rear antilock brake system (RABS), referring to the fact that only the rear wheels had ABS.

example. The major difference between this system and a conventional brake system is the fact that there is no mechanical connection between the brake pedal and the wheels. The brake pedal input is monitored and sent by electrical signals to the modulator, which usually uses a pump and high-pressure accumulator (HPA) to send the fluid to the wheel using several solenoids.

Regenerative braking, also known as "regen" brakes, use magnetism to help slow a vehicle. A motor/generator is typically mounted around the flywheel. It can start the vehicle and also provide braking action while it helps recharge the battery.

When in brake mode, the operation could be described as the opposite of a motor. When the brakes are applied on a vehicle with regen brakes, the drive motor is used as a generator and the magnetism causes the shaft to be more difficult to turn, resulting in braking action. This magnetism is used to recharge the vehicle's drive battery pack. Vehicles such as the Toyota Prius have used this concept for many years. Because of the lightweight construction of this vehicle, the regen brake

The Possibility of Mandatory Maintenance

As vehicles have progressed and more electronics have been added to replace mechanical functions, they have become more like the systems used in aviation. There, mandatory maintenance is required, even on private aircraft.

When autonomous vehicles are common on the roads, it may be necessary for mandatory maintenance to become a reality in the automotive world. For example, a wire harness leading to a caliper may need to be replaced at a specified time or mileage interval. The decision may not be left up to the owner of the vehicle. ∎

system is capable of supplying most of the brake force, so the base brakes often last a long time if the vehicle is driven normally. Some have reported that the brakes lasted the life of the vehicle.

A new type of brake system is currently being tested in Europe. Known as Electronic Wedge Braking (EWB), the system uses disc brakes with a sliding caliper that is actuated by electric motors rather than a hydraulic piston. A sliding plate with raised humps on it is moved back and forth by two electric motors. The inboard brake pad also has raised humps, but the valleys of the humps of the pads are in contact with the high spots on the sliding plate. When braking is needed, one of the motors slides

the plate, which causes the humps to apply the inboard pad to the spinning rotor. As contact is made, the pad can move with the rotor, which increases brake force by wedging action against the plate. The outboard pad is applied in the usual manner when the caliper slides on its pins or guides.

This design eliminates many expensive, heavy components such as the brake booster, master cylinder, ABS unit, lines, and hoses. The calipers must have a wire harness instead of a brake hose, which could be subject to wear when the suspension moves and steering takes place. It may also become brittle over time or due to cold temperatures and require replacement more frequently than a rubber hose.

Regenerative braking is used on many hybrid and electric vehicles. Most still use a downsized conventional brake system, but the bulk of the braking is accomplished by using the vehicle's propulsion motor as a generator during stopping. The generator recharges the batteries during normal stopping. If additional braking is required, the conventional brake system is also applied.

This is the main drive battery from a Tesla. Most hybrid and electric vehicles use regenerative braking to slow the vehicle and recharge the battery when the brakes are applied normally. Heavy braking causes the conventional brakes at the wheels to help stop the vehicle.

BRAKE SYSTEM COMPONENTS

The modern automotive and light truck brake system is made of many components working together to achieve effective control while slowing or bringing the vehicle to a safe stop.

When you press the brake pedal in a vehicle with manual brakes, linkage connects the mechanical force to hydraulic pistons, which pressurize sealed systems of lines, hoses, and output pistons with high-pressure fluid that applies the friction material to the spinning rotor or drum to stop the vehicle. Think of a cylinder type of squirt gun. Pressing on the plunger causes water to squirt from the other end. If this end were connected by a hose to another cylinder full of water the same size, the movement of the input plunger would cause equal movement at the output plunger. This movement is used to apply the brake pads or shoes to stop the vehicle. If the output piston diameter were twice that of the input, the output would apply twice the force, but it would move half the distance.

On a vehicle, the cylinder applied by your foot is known as the master cylinder and the cylinder that applies the friction at each wheel is known as a caliper or wheel cylinder. This is referred to as the hydraulic system. No matter how long the lines are, as long as they are full of fluid there will be immediate movement at the output for every movement you make at the input.

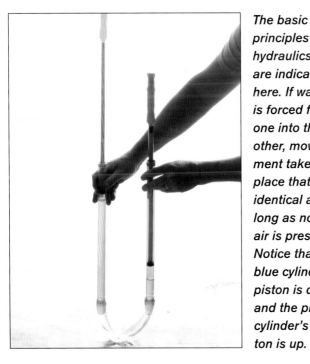

The basic principles of hydraulics are indicated here. If water is forced from one into the other, movement takes place that is identical as long as no air is present. Notice that the blue cylinder's piston is down and the pink cylinder's piston is up.

When the pink cylinder's piston is pressed down, the blue cylinder's piston comes up the exact same amount. No matter how long the brake line or hose connecting the two cylinders is, the same movement takes place if the cylinders are the same diameter and no air is present. If the input cylinder is smaller than the output, the output cylinder moves less but has greater force. This is how the hydraulic circuit between the master cylinder and a brake caliper operates.

A caliper contains a cylinder with at least one piston that clamps two brake pads around the rotor. A wheel cylinder is a cylinder with a piston at each end that push the two brake shoes into the spinning drum. In both cases, the pistons press the friction material against the spinning component at each wheel to stop the vehicle.

Steel tubing and high-pressure hoses route the pressurized fluid to each wheel. The fluid must not contain any air so that all the input can travel to the outputs. Fluid cannot compress but air can and it affects brake force and pedal height. If there's air in the system, the brake pedal feels spongy and may drop because you are compressing the air when you press down. Brake bleeding is the term used for the process of expelling air from the system.

Understanding the Pieces

The following is a description of each component in the brake system.

The entire hydraulic system is filled with brake fluid and linked with steel tubing and high-pressure hoses and must be absent of air because air can compress, causing ineffective braking and a low, spongy brake pedal.

Brake Pedal

The brake pedal is on a pivot pin and lever action is used to increase the force applied by your foot. The linkage or rod from the pedal to the power booster or master cylinder can be adjusted. The brake light switch, or pedal travel sensor, is often located near the pedal lever to monitor its position. It turns on the brake lights and may also be an input to various other systems on the vehicle such as ABS, cruise control, or an electronic brake module.

Power Booster

The booster is mounted on the bulkhead (firewall) and uses vacuum or power steering pressure to increase the pedal force going into the master cylinder. The input to the booster is supplied by mechanical foot force from the brake pedal rod on the other side of the firewall. The output is transmitted through a pushrod into the master cylinder. Sometimes this pushrod is adjustable and the proper length is critical to prevent brake lockup or excessive pedal travel.

In a real brake system, high-pressure cylinders and lines are used, but the concept is no different than in the illustrations. The input piston in the master cylinder is applied when you press on the brake pedal and fluid flows to pistons of different sizes to produce the force needed at that wheel. Disc brakes require high force, so a larger piston is used. Drum brakes require less force but more movement to apply them, so a smaller piston is used.

The brake pedal is a lever that presses on a rod leading to the master cylinder. Mechanical advantage is obtained because the lever is offset. Most brake pedal linkage is adjustable. If the vehicle has power brakes, a power booster is located between the brake pedal and master cylinder to increase the force and reduce pedal effort.

The power booster uses vacuum or power steering pressure to increase the force from the brake pedal to the master cylinder. Most modern vehicles use power brakes, which greatly reduces the effort needed to apply the brakes. The engine must be running for the power brakes to function. Should the engine die, a backup system ensures at least two assisted stops. The master cylinder receives the force from the power booster (arrow) and uses pistons to force brake fluid under pressure to the wheels.

Master Cylinder

The master cylinder bolts to the booster and contains two pistons that move when the brake pedal is applied. One piston supplies fluid to two wheels and the other piston serves the other two wheels. A reservoir of fluid above the pistons supplies reserve fluid for the system. When your foot is off the brake, the master cylinder allows fluid to flow from the wheels into the reservoir. This is necessary because the fluid expands when it heats up and must be allowed to escape from the wheels or the brakes may lock up. The passages inside the master cylinder responsible for this fluid escape are called vent ports.

Brake Lines

Metal brake lines lead from the master cylinder to flexible hoses

Brake lines are usually made of high-strength steel to withstand hydraulic pressures that can exceed 1,600 pounds. Special fittings are used at each connection to ensure safety and eliminate leakage. Lines are subjected to harsh operating conditions under the vehicle, so rust is a common problem that can lead to the need to replace the lines.

Older vehicles used mechanical valves to vary the hydraulic pressure to the wheels during braking. A proportioning valve in the line to the rear brakes reduces rear wheel lockup during panic stops and a metering valve in the line to the front brakes delays the front disc brakes long enough for the rear drum brakes to apply. This reduces nosedive during braking. A pressure differential switch turns on the red brake warning lamp if a leak occurs. Most of these functions are performed electronically on current models.

at the wheels. Some vehicles have hydraulic valves between the master cylinder and the wheels. Most modern vehicles also incorporate an ABS modulator in the lines between the master cylinder and the wheels, which is controlled by a processor.

Brake Hoses

At the end of the metal lines, rubber brake hoses are used to allow for wheel movement during steering and suspension operation. These hoses connect the metal lines to the calipers or wheel cylinders and route the high-pressure fluid to the calipers and wheel cylinders during brake operation.

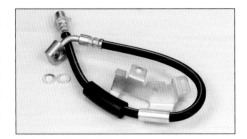

Flexible brake hoses are used between the steel brake lines and the wheels to accommodate steering and suspension movement. These hoses contain multiple layers of tubing and high-strength fabric to withstand the high hydraulic pressures in the system. Careful inspection is required to determine if cracks have developed, which are an indication that replacement is needed.

Brake Calipers

A brake caliper contains at least one piston that converts hydraulic pressure from the lines and hoses to the mechanical movement needed to force the brake pads into the spinning rotor, which slows or stops the vehicle. When the brakes are released, the piston seal slightly retracts the piston to reduce drag and improve fuel economy.

A brake caliper contains one or more pistons that clamp the brake pads against the spinning rotor when the brakes are applied. It contains anti-rattle hardware to reduce brake noise. Most calipers slide or float on pins or ledges that must be clean and lubricated to ensure proper operation.

Wheel Cylinders

Wheel cylinders contain pistons that convert the hydraulic pressure from the lines and hoses to mechanical force to apply the brake shoes to the inside of the drum to slow the vehicle. When the brakes are released, springs inside the drum pull the shoes away from the drum.

A wheel cylinder is used to apply the brake shoes inside of a drum brake system. It contains two pistons that extend outward due to the hydraulic pressure generated when the brake pedal is applied. This movement is transferred to the brake shoes, which are forced into the spinning drum.

Brake Pads

Brake pads have friction material attached to a plate of metal. A brake pad is located on each side of the rotor. One is known as the inboard pad (nearest the piston) and the other is known as the outboard pad. They are squeezed with high force against the rotor by the caliper piston(s) when the brakes are applied.

Brake pads are relatively small sections of friction material attached to a metal backing plate. They are placed on each side of the rotor and clamped against it by the caliper when the brakes are applied. They provide very effective braking and handle heat well.

Disc Brake Hardware

Disc brakes use metal slides, shims, and anti-rattle clips to minimize brake noise and ensure proper operation during brake apply and release. Some are insulated on rubber bushings.

Because brake squeal is a byproduct of the vibration caused by brake systems, engineers generally use anti-rattle clips and springs to minimize the noise generated by disc brake systems. A shim between the brake pad and caliper or piston may also be used to reduce the potential for brake noise.

Brake Shoes

Brake shoes are C-shaped and are lined with friction material. The two inside of each drum are forced against the inside of the brake drum when the brakes are applied. They are also sometimes referred to as brake linings.

Brake shoes perform the same task as brake pads. Friction material is attached to the shoe with rivets or a bonding process. When the shoes contact the drum during braking, they increase their force by wedging into the drum.

Drum Brake Hardware

Several springs and linkages are used to keep the brake shoes in proper position and also serve to retract the brake shoes when the brake pedal is released. In addition, automatic adjusters are used to maintain proper brake pedal height as the shoe material wears. Some of the hardware is also used to apply the parking brake when the vehicle is parked.

Rotors

Brake rotors are connected to the wheels and rotate as the wheels turn. When the brake pads clamp around the rotor, the rotor is slowed or stopped. Heat is generated and must be released through conduction and radiation.

Drums

The brake drums also have the vehicle's wheels bolted to them and they rotate as the wheels turn. When the brake shoes are pressed into the inside of the drum during brake operation, the drum is slowed or stopped.

Brake parts on older cars were made of heavy cast iron and steel. Modern cars use more aluminum and plastic. Due to reduced mass, brake noise is more common today than ever. It is imperative to do the job right using quality parts or brake noise and other problems may occur.

Beyond the Basics

In addition to these basic components found in nearly every brake system, the vehicle could also be equipped with various valves and ABS components. As systems have progressed, the brake system is the basis for several other systems including the traction control system (TCS), vehicle stability control (VSC), ABS, ADAS, and stability control. These systems will continue to be key components of future vehicles, even autonomous vehicles. Chapter 9: ABS, ADAS, and Related Systems contains more information on these systems.

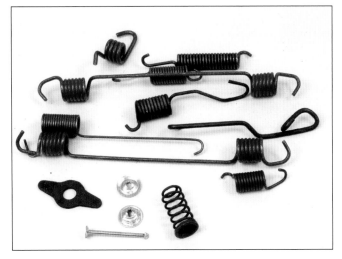

Drum brakes use hold-down and return springs as well as automatic adjuster and parking brake components. These components are part of a hardware and adjuster kit when a brake overhaul is needed. Due to heat, these components should be replaced during servicing.

Brake rotors are made of iron and generally have cooling fins when used on the front of a vehicle. Some rear rotors are solid without cooling fins. The brake pads are squeezed around the rotor surface by the caliper when the brakes are applied, which slows or stops the vehicle.

The brake drum covers the shoes that expand into it when the brakes are applied. Because the drum fits over the wheel studs, this action slows the vehicle.

DISC BRAKE SYSTEMS

Caution 1: The information in this chapter is based on general knowledge and may not be specific to your vehicle. Specific information is available in the factory service manual for your vehicle, which should be consulted for torque specifications, procedures, and safety concerns.

Caution 2: Some newer vehicles with electronic brake systems require a scan tool for servicing. See "New Technology Precautions" at the end of this chapter before servicing a vehicle with an electronic brake system.

Most modern vehicles use disc brakes on the front and disc or drum brakes on the rear. Because the front brakes do as much as 80–90 percent of the work when stopping,

they tend to wear out quicker, requiring more frequent replacement than the rear brakes.

Drum brakes were used on the front and rear of cars into the 1970s. Since then, disc brakes have taken the place of drums on the front and in many cases on the rears too because they offer many advantages over drum brakes. They are much better equipped to dissipate the heat generated by modern vehicles, are easier to service, and are better suited for operation in wet conditions. They also self-adjust more reliably than drum brakes and resist brake fade (brake fade is the term used by engineers to explain a temporary loss of braking, usually due to heat). A drum can expand away from

the brake shoes during heavy use, causing a lower brake pedal, but disc brake rotor expansion does not cause this condition when hot. Disc brakes also can shed gases and wear particles better than drum brakes and are less likely to cause the vehicle to pull to one side during stopping.

Today's front-wheel-drive vehicles, SUVs, and light trucks have most of the weight up front, which is why engineers design brake systems to have more brake "bias" to the front end. If the same amount of brake force was present on the rear as the front during a hard stop, the rear brakes could lock up. This could lead to a loss of control, especially if the lockup occurs during a turn.

Disc brakes are common due to their advantages over drum brakes, but drum brakes are still found on the rear of some vehicles. Every year, more vehicles are produced with disc brakes on all four corners.

The pressure from this C-clamp is the same on both sides of the wood, even though the threaded shaft only presses on one side. One of Newton's laws is that "For every action, there is an equal and opposite reaction."

Operation

Imagine a large C-clamp around a 2x4 board. As you tighten the threaded shaft, both sides of the board are squeezed by the clamp the same amount, even though you are only tightening the screw against one side. Sir Isaac Newton stated: "For every action, there is an equal and opposite reaction."

Calipers

The modern disc brake system is designed to clamp the brake pads against the spinning rotor to slow or stop the vehicle when you apply the brakes, much like the C-clamp. This device is known as a caliper. Hydraulic pressure from the master cylinder is developed when you press the brake pedal. This pressure moves the piston(s) in the caliper toward the pad(s) just like tightening the drive screw on the clamp.

On sliding or floating calipers, the piston(s) extends out of the caliper when the brake pedal is applied, causing one brake pad to make contact with the rotor (the action). As soon as contact is made, the caliper slides the other way (the reaction), which causes the other pad to make contact with the rotor.

This action and reaction clamps the pads onto the spinning rotor to slow or stop the vehicle. This design is called a sliding or floating caliper because that is exactly what it does. Sliding calipers ride on metal tracks, and floating calipers ride on pins or bolts with special seals and lubricants. It is easy to understand the concept if you visualize the C-clamp's operation.

After you remove your foot from the brake pedal, a square-cut seal around the piston flexes back and acts as a return spring. It slightly retracts the piston so that the pads move away from the rotor just enough to allow free rotation. This ring sits in a groove in the bore around the piston; so, it is not actually mounted on the piston like an engine piston ring. The piston can be made of steel, aluminum, or a phenolic material. Phenolic is a synthetic material with superior heat resistance.

A caliper consists of a housing with a cylinder for hydraulic pressure to push the piston into the brake pad and into contact with the rotor. A seal in the bore of the cylinder allows the piston to build pressure and force the pads into the rotor. A dust seal (arrow) keeps out contaminants.

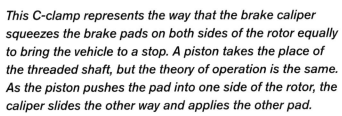

This C-clamp represents the way that the brake caliper squeezes the brake pads on both sides of the rotor equally to bring the vehicle to a stop. A piston takes the place of the threaded shaft, but the theory of operation is the same. As the piston pushes the pad into one side of the rotor, the caliper slides the other way and applies the other pad.

This caliper piston is made of steel but can also be made of aluminum or phenolic material. It rides in a seal in the cylinder bore. Because it has a larger diameter than the master cylinder piston, a hydraulic advantage exists, which means that a greater force is applied to the brake pads to help stop the vehicle.

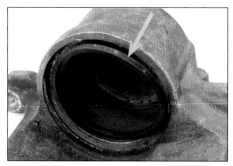

The sealing ring (arrow) in a caliper piston is different than that of a ring on a piston in an engine. It is in a groove in the bore of the cylinder rather than on the piston itself. The groove it rides in is chamfered so that the seal flexes when the brakes are applied.

The sealing ring around the caliper piston is known as a square-cut seal. After the piston moves out to apply the pads during braking, it is retracted as the seal relaxes to its normal shape after being deflected. This reduces brake drag and improves fuel economy.

The brake caliper holds the pads in position and is bolted to the steering knuckle. A separate bracket may be used between the caliper and the steering knuckle on some applications. Stamped steel metal slides or guides and anti-vibration hardware or clips sit between the pads and caliper or bracket. This hardware often puts a small amount of spring tension on the pads to hold them in position to reduce vibration and prevent brake squeals, squeaks, and rattles.

Most disc brake systems use shims on the back of the pads, sheet metal guides, and spring clips to reduce brake pad rattle and squeal. Without these components, the pads would likely cause unwanted noise.

Most vehicles use a sliding or floating caliper design with either one or two pistons on one side of the rotor. It is imperative that the caliper slides freely for the brakes to work properly and the pads to wear evenly. The advantages to this design are that it is lightweight, easy to manufacture, low cost, and not prone to leakage. The disadvantages are that

A brake pad contains a specific formulation of components to provide adequate stopping with a minimum of noise, dusting, and wear. Various formulations are used to handle the demands of heavy loads and heat or the extremes of emergency vehicles and race vehicles.

This single-piston floating caliper is a common design. It is lightweight and easy to service while still able to supply good stopping power and heat dissipation. A growing number of calipers are made of aluminum to reduce weight.

Some vehicles use a dual-piston floating caliper. The pistons are on one side of the rotor, so the caliper must still slide freely to engage the outboard pads during braking just as the single-piston caliper does. The dual-piston design can apply more force evenly across the pad for greater stopping power.

flexing can occur because the piston(s) is only on one side of the rotor. This can cause tapered pad wear. The slides can become contaminated and drag, leading to noise and one pad wearing more than the other.

A few vehicles use a fixed caliper, meaning that it does not slide. It has one or more pistons on each side of the pads that apply at the same time

This is a fixed caliper, meaning that it is rigidly mounted and does not slide like a floating caliper. It has pistons on both sides of the rotor and a passage or transfer tube for fluid to flow between the two halves. Fixed calipers are generally found on older vehicles and performance cars.

when the brake pedal is pressed. These calipers are usually heavier and have more potential for leaks, but they are known for excellent stopping and extremely even pad wear. Their weight dampens noise, and this generally results in minimal brake squeak or squeal. The greater weight is also a factor in vehicle handling. Because the brake caliper is "unsprung," its weight has a greater negative effect on suspension operation versus "sprung" weight. This can be mitigated through the use of aluminum and more expensive alloys.

Fixed calipers were popular on performance cars in the 1970s but are not as common today. They are found on older vehicles, some modern exotics, and high-performance racing applications. Some of the latest GMC and Chevrolet light trucks are equipped with fixed calipers.

Low-Drag Calipers

Because of government Corporate Average Fuel Economy (CAFE) and emission control standards, low-drag calipers were designed some years ago. Cars of the 1970s

with disc brakes did not have calipers that retracted much, so they dragged the pads on the rotors until flex in the components caused enough "knock back" to free the rotors. If you jacked up a car in those days and attempted to spin the wheel, you probably had to pry the caliper piston back a bit to allow the wheel to spin. This wasn't considered to be a problem, however, until fuel prices increased in 1973. Engineers knew that a wheel that was easier to spin improved fuel economy, so low-drag calipers entered the scene.

A special square-cut seal around the caliper piston in the bore flexes when the brakes are applied. When the brakes are released, the seal flexes back, which pulls the piston back away from the pads like a spring. This results in free-wheel rotation much quicker and, as a result, better fuel economy. It also likely improves pad life due to less dragging on the rotors. When you use less fuel, the vehicle has lower emissions.

Quick Take-up Master Cylinders

Some manufacturers developed master cylinders that supplied more fluid volume when the brake pedal was first applied to counteract the extra piston retraction from the low-drag caliper design. Without the redesign, the pedal required more movement before the brakes applied. These master cylinders are known as "quick take-up" or "fast fill" master cylinders and usually have a larger bore feeding the primary chamber to get fluid to those wheels quicker and maintain an acceptable pedal height.

Parking Brake for Rear Discs

If disc brakes are used on the rear of a vehicle, they operate just like

This rear caliper uses an integral parking brake that moves the piston into the pad when the cable is applied. It uses a corkscrew design inside the piston that is prone to rust and binding. The piston must be rotated as it is pressed back into the caliper with a special tool prior to pad replacement.

Some rear disc parking brakes use a small set of brake shoes inside of a drum cast inside the rotor. This is referred to as the rotor hat section. These shoes should never wear out because the rotor should be stationary when the parking brake is applied.

the front brakes but they are likely smaller and have the parking brake system built into them. Some applications use a corkscrew-like shaft that is actuated by a cable or electric motor drive to apply the parking brake. Others may have a small drum system inside the rotor for parking brake application, which is more effective due to self-energizing brake shoe action.

Brake Pads

Brake pads are relatively small pieces of friction material attached to a steel backing plate that press against the rotor under hydraulic force. A process known as sintering is used to make brake pads. Most pads are composed of several elements compressed together and heated in a mold.

The composition of the formula used varies from vehicle to vehicle and among different manufacturers. It can possess high percentages of different compounds such as organic material, semimetallic particles, ceramic, carbon metallic, Kevlar, or silicone carbide. Some pads excel in heat control, braking ability, and even reduce wheel dusting. Some wear faster than others but may offer more aggressive braking for racing or heavy loads. Other components include binders (glue) and fillers. Sometimes even ground-up walnut shells are used in the mix as a filler!

Brake engineers design tailored systems for the needs of each specific vehicle platform, often with a special patented mix of ingredients in the brake pad formula. Vehicle engineers must meet strict Department of Transportation (DOT) standards for stopping distance, and they often stamp the heat-handling ability onto to the edge of the pad or shoe. This code gives an indication of how much heat the friction material can handle when both hot and cold. This is called an edge code and is classified using letters of the alphabet, with higher letters meaning better heat handling (GG could handle more heat than EE, for example).

Most pads today are bonded, meaning that the friction surface is attached to a steel backing plate using high pressure and heat in a

Some older disc brake designs used a brake pad with the friction material riveted to the steel backing plate. This type of pad cannot wear as much as a bonded pad without the rivets causing damage to the brake rotor. Some pad manufacturers placed a thin insulator between the friction material and backing plate for quieter operation.

Most brake pads in use today have the friction material bonded to the steel backing plate. During manufacturing, friction material is placed under high pressure and heat to form it and bond it to the backing plate.

Some manufacturers have holes through the steel backing plate so that friction material can flow through during manufacturing. This helps keep the friction material in place. One well-known manufacturer has a thin friction surface on the other side that acts as a very effective shim for noise reduction.

mold during manufacturing. Pad backing plates may have a rough surface with fish-hook-like teeth where friction is bonded to help the pad material remain on the plate. Older designs used rivets to attach the friction "puck" to the backing plate. Some newer designs have holes in the plate; friction material is pressed into it during manufacturing to help hold it to the plate during operation. Some even have a thin layer of friction material on the backside of the pad to act as a shim for noise control.

Pad Materials and Applications

A pickup truck designed to haul a 36-foot fifth-wheel camper that weighs 12,000 pounds would likely be equipped with semimetallic brake pads from the factory. This composition includes a high level of metallic particles in the formulation that are extremely good at drawing heat away from the rotors and conducting it into the suspension system and wheels.

For severe-duty applications such as police, ambulance, or racing, a pad containing even more

Brake pad manufacturers often use chamfered edges and slots in the friction surface to reduce vibration and wear particle accumulation. Both can cause brake noise.

metallic particles is available, often called severe-duty or carbon-metallic. These pads work well on extremely hot surfaces but do not grip well on cold rotors, so this formulation is not a good choice for a small lightweight sedan. Severe-duty pads also tend to be noisier and cause more extreme rotor wear due to their high metal content and aggressive nature.

German vehicles often use silicone-carbide formulations, which are also aggressive and can cause rotor wear and high wheel dusting, but the benefit is excellent stopping power. It is not uncommon for some German vehicles to require new rotors during every brake job because the aggressive friction wears the rotors.

Lighter weight vehicle applications used organic and asbestos formulations years ago. Asbestos was found to cause cancer, so it has been replaced with non-asbestos formulations. Some light-duty pads also contain copper particles. Brake pads containing copper have come under scrutiny because of the copper dust potentially being washed into drains on the street and entering the water supply.

Ceramic formulations are extremely popular on lighter weight applications. They are generally quieter and shed a lighter color dust, which improves wheel appearance. However, they tend to be less able to conduct heat away from the rotor. They act more like a barrier or insulator. This can cause the rotor to run hotter, so they are not a good choice for the truck pulling the camper mentioned earlier, even though less dust may be seen on that vehicle's wheels. Some pads deposit a darker color dust and wear away some metal from the rotor for them to work properly. The bottom line is that it is not wise to

sacrifice braking ability when pulling a heavy load to have cleaner wheels!

There are no standards for the percentage of compounds required to call a pad a certain name, such as Kevlar or ceramic. Advertisers often use these as a way to help their products sell, even though the percentage may be extremely low.

There is no perfect pad for all applications just as there is no tire that can do everything for every demand. If a tire can last 80,000 miles, it will not be able to give good traction in rain and snow. If it is aggressive for off-road use, it will probably be extremely noisy on the highway. If it has amazing grip around turns, it probably won't last long. Nearly everything on a vehicle is a compromise. That also applies to fuel efficiency versus speed. Fast sports cars typically use a lot of fuel. Little fuel-efficient cars aren't fast.

In the same way, each brake pad has its own strengths and weaknesses, and the choice of pad material should not be based solely on price or how clean the wheels remain. On the internet, you can find pads for the same vehicle from $15 to $115, so it might be confusing to determine which pad is right for your application. Most quality pad manufacturers have catalog listings that show the factory formulation in bold print and options such as severe-duty or

ceramic in lighter print. For the average driver, it is probably best to stay as close to the factory formulation as possible because the original equipment manufacturer (OEM) engineers likely spent a lot of time and money to decide that they were the best! Pads are sold in axle sets, so one box does both the left and right sides.

Some pads have chamfered edges and slots that are intended to reduce noise from vibration or to channel away gases and wear particles. Replacement pads may differ in appearance from originals. If they are from a trusted manufacturer, they might perform better than the OEM design, but be sure they fit properly and are listed for your vehicle in their catalog.

Even though the original OEM is held to strict government Federal Motor Vehicle Safety Standards (FMVSS 135) regarding original equipment brake performance, the aftermarket does not have many restrictions on brake pad material or design. It is best to stay with a name brand and not to shop for brake pads based on price alone.

Rotors

Most brake rotors are a one-piece design made of cast iron or a composite design using a steel plate with a cast-iron friction surface. Performance applications,

Many performance vehicles come from the factory with carbon-ceramic rotors. The main advantages are superior braking and weight reduction for handling, performance, and fuel economy. Less unsprung weight means better handling. Less overall weight (approximately 50 pounds) means improved performance, better fuel mileage, and lower emissions.

Use Caution with Brake Fluid

Some technicians prefer to wear disposable gloves when working around brakes and brake fluid. You may not have the same "feel" at your fingertips when handling small parts such as copper washers, but disposable gloves are relatively thin so that they can work. They are usually available in boxes of 100 for less than $10. Caution: Brake fluid is extremely damaging to paint, so be extremely careful when you are working with it. ∎

Vehicles may be equipped with drilled and slotted rotors to reduce heat and for channeling wear particles away from the rotor surface. Aftermarket brake upgrade kits with these features are also available for many applications.

such as late-model Corvettes, use carbon-ceramic rotors, which are not metal. They are expensive but handle heat extremely well and weigh about 11 pounds less than a comparable cast-iron rotor. This reduces unsprung weight, improving handling and ride and reducing overall vehicle weight, which improves performance and reduces emissions.

Often the front rotors are a vented design with cooling fins between the two friction surfaces. If your vehicle is equipped with rear disc brakes, the rotor can also be a one-piece plate without cooling fins because they don't have to deal with the heat that the front brakes do.

Some performance vehicles are equipped with drilled and/or slotted rotors from the factory. This is to assist with channeling gases and wear material away from the contact surfaces between the rotor and pad and improve brake performance.

Aftermarket components to add these features to your existing vehicle are available. Purchase from a reputable source to be sure that you are getting an actual improvement in brake performance. Performance systems may include larger diameter rotors and upgraded calipers and can be quite expensive.

Some may look good through the wheel but actually cause the brakes to run hotter due to a reduction in rotor mass. They could just be the factory type of rotor with holes drilled in them.

Inspection and Diagnosis

Disc brakes can become worn without displaying warning signs. There will be no change in pedal height or feel and the vehicle continues to stop until the friction surface is completely worn away. Some vehicles have audible wear sensors attached to the brake pads that make contact with the rotor surface, causing a high-pitched squeal when the

It is sometimes difficult to view the condition of the pads and rotors without removing the wheel. This is especially true of the backside of the rotor and inboard pads. Some applications have a full backing plate on the inboard side of the rotor to protect it from contamination, which greatly restricts visibility.

pads are almost worn out. This is usually heard when the brakes are not applied.

You may be able to get a partial view of the outboard pad and rotor surface through the wheel, but a

Most brake pads have a metal wear sensor (arrow) that is designed to scrape against the rotor when the pads are almost worn out. Its purpose is to alert the driver that brake service may be required soon.

This is an example of a brake pad that was worn past the friction surface and into the steel backing plate. Most of the time, the rotor is damaged to the point of requiring replacement.

Most luxury and German vehicles have electronic wear sensors. This type of sensor completes a circuit to ground when the pads are nearing the end of their life. A warning lamp on the instrument panel is illuminated so that the owner knows that brake service will be required soon.

thorough inspection requires wheel removal to get a good look at the entire system because a backing plate hides the inboard pad and rotor surface from view.

If the sensor is ignored, the metal backing plate or rivets make contact with the rotor face when the friction material wears away and causes severe damage to the rotor surface. If the metal-to-metal condition continues, the area where the pads contact the rotor can become completely worn away and the caliper piston can come out of the rotor, causing hydraulic failure and complete loss of braking on that circuit.

Some high-end vehicles have electronic sensors that cause a warning lamp on the instrument panel to appear when the pads are nearing the end of their life. This design gen-erally uses a brush-like material to ground a circuit through the rotor.

Another telltale sign of brake pad wear is low brake fluid level in the master cylinder reservoir. If the fluid level is extremely low, a brake indicator lamp may illuminate on the instrument panel.

Low fluid level in the master cylinder is caused by a hydraulic system leak or disc brake pad wear. As the pads wear and their thickness diminishes, fluid must take up the void behind the caliper pistons, which leads to less fluid in the master cylinder. This master cylinder has a sensor (arrow) that turns on a dash light when the fluid level is low.

Ignoring the warning signs can lead to more expensive repairs. This rotor was severely damaged because the friction material on the pad was completely worn away and metal-to-metal contact was the result. Much noise resulted but was apparently ignored.

The Test Drive

The first step in assessing a disc brake system is a thorough test drive. Listen for noises and watch for pulling to the left or right when the brakes are applied. Observe the brake pedal height and feel of the pedal when stopping. See if the force required to stop the vehicle is abnormal. If the pedal moves up and down (pulsates), the rotors may need attention. If the pedal is unusually low, the drum brake system may need adjustment or repair. There could also be an issue with the ABS system.

On disc brakes, a low pedal does not result from worn brake pads because they are self-adjusting as fluid takes up the space behind the piston as the pads wear. A pull to one side during braking could be the result of a restricted brake hose, caliper, or pad issue or even a loose or worn wheel bearing. It could even be caused by a steering or suspension problem.

If the pedal is hard and the vehicle is difficult to stop, you may have a power booster failure or low engine vacuum.

If the pedal is spongy or soft, you may have air in the fluid. Some vehicles have hydroboost brake assist that receives fluid from the power steering pump to assist in stopping. Be sure the power steering fluid level is correct and the hoses are intact.

Visual Inspection

After the test drive, open the hood and wipe away any dirt that may have accumulated around the lid of the master cylinder. Remove the lid and observe the level of the fluid. You may be able to see through the reservoir on some applications without removing the lid. The fluid should fall between the minimum and maximum markings. If the fluid is low, it could be an indication of a leak or the brake pads could be worn.

Don't let any fluid from the lid or your hands come in contact with any painted surface. Brake fluid damages painted surfaces. If you do accidently get brake fluid on a painted surface, flush the surface immediately with plenty of water.

Now it's time to remove the front wheels to get a good look at the disc brakes. You may be able to see the outboard surface of the rotor and the outboard pad through the wheel, but to perform a thorough inspection, the wheel must be removed. Often a backing plate is used, which can limit visual inspection of the backside of the rotor surface and the inboard pads. Some pickups and SUVs that are not often used develop a layer of rust on the backside of the rotor, which greatly affects braking ability. This can easily be missed if the wheels are not removed during inspection.

Raising the Vehicle

To check the front brakes, you first chock both rear wheels, making sure the vehicle is in park or in gear with the parking brake applied and the engine off. If you're using hand tools, remove the front wheel covers or center caps (if used) and loosen the wheel fasteners slightly.

Carefully raise the vehicle using an appropriate method such as a floor jack placed as specified by your vehicle's manufacturer.

When the vehicle is high enough to allow the front wheels to be removed, place jack stands under the vehicle and lower the floor jack to allow the vehicle weight to rest on the stands.

Be sure that you raise the vehicle per your vehicle manufacturer's guidelines. The American Lift Institute (ALI) issues a guide that lists all vehicles and their lift points. Lifting information for your specific vehicle might also be available online.

A floor jack with adequate capacity should be placed at the proper lifting point for your vehicle and carefully lifted high enough to allow wheel removal. Do not use the jack that came with your vehicle to support it while servicing your brake system.

Wheel chocks should be placed on both sides of the opposing wheel when jacking up a vehicle. Also be sure that the vehicle is in park or in gear and the parking brake is applied before raising the vehicle. If you are using hand tools to remove the wheel fasteners, slightly loosen them before raising the wheel off the ground.

A jack stand with adequate capacity must be used to support the weight of the vehicle prior to beginning brake inspection or service. If the jack stand is placed under the vehicle as a safety backup and the jack is supporting the weight, it could be crushed if the jack should fail. This is referred to as "shock loading." Jack stands are not rated for this type of load.

Remove the wheel fasteners and lift the wheel from the hub. Wheels are heavy, so be careful. Some manufacturers recommend marking the stud position and reinstalling the wheel in the same position.

Remove the wheel fasteners. Most vehicles use nuts that require one of the following socket sizes: 3/4, 13/16, or 7/8 inch or 17, 19, 21, or 22 mm. German vehicles and Saturn vehicles use wheel bolts instead of nuts, and most require a 17-mm socket for service. Some trucks and SUVs use larger lug nuts that require a larger socket. Some older vehicles have left-handed threads on the driver-side wheel studs.

If you are using hand tools, you may need to have an assistant hold down the brake pedal as you remove the fasteners to keep the wheel from spinning. Do not attempt to work on a vehicle if it is lifted unsafely. Don't use the jack that came with your vehicle or wood blocks to support the vehicle during brake service. Only an automotive jack stand rated for the load should be used.

After the two front wheels are removed, you have a much better view of the disc brake system.

Brake Pad Inspection

The thickness of the friction material on most new brake pads is 1/4 to 1/2 inch. Every manufacturer has replacement guidelines for thickness and some states have vehicle inspections to ensure that the thickness is safe for vehicle operation. Some allow as little as 1/16 inch on bonded pads or 1/8 inch on riveted pads before the vehicle is rejected. Special tools are available to measure pad thickness on the vehicle using color coding. Some are able to obtain the actual thickness remaining without removing the pad first.

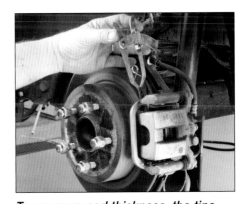

To measure pad thickness, the tips of a scaled tool are placed between the rotor and the pad backing plate. The scale displays the remaining pad thickness in increments of 1/32 inch.

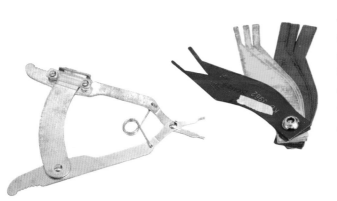

Several tools are available to measure brake pad thickness while the pads are still on the vehicle. The color-coded gauges indicate a range of thicknesses. The other tool has a scale to read exact dimensions.

The color-coded "go-no-go" gauge is placed between the rotor surface and the pad backing plate like a feeler gauge. The color codes indicate whether the remaining pad thickness represents an immediate concern or not. The green gauges are the thickest and the red ones are the thinnest.

Here a color-coded gauge is in use. The yellow gauge slides in and out easily with light drag, indicating that the pad still has some life left.

Look for cracks that may affect operation or contamination from brake fluid or grease. If found, the pads should be replaced, not just cleaned. Grease can be absorbed into the pad structure. Pads can also be overheated. Generally you see evidence of this on the rotor surface in the form of blue, black, or brown heat marks or hot spots. If this found, rotor replacement is required.

Excessive uneven (wedge shaped) wear or one pad wearing more than the other could mean caliper slide issues. If the vehicle has a sliding or floating design and the outboard pad is worn more than the inboard, the slides are dirty. If the inboard pad is worn more than the outboard, the slides are seized. If you do not address these issues, the new pads will develop the same wear patterns.

Brake Noise

Unfortunately brake noise occurs from time to time. It is the most common reason that professional brake shops have vehicle "comebacks."

Doing the job right and taking the proper steps during service minimizes the possibility of brake noise, but because all brakes vibrate and vibration can be audible, noises can happen. The goal of an automotive brake engineer is to make the frequency of the vibration outside of the range of human hearing.

Unusual weather dry spells can contribute to brake noise. Be sure to use new hardware installed correctly and proper lubricant in all the right places. A coarse rotor surface creates "mountain peaks" where the new pads ride. This reduces surface contact, which causes higher pedal effort, excess wheel dusting, and noise until the surfaces smooth out and comply with each other. The smoothness of the rotor face is measured in roughness average (RA); the lower the number, the smoother the face.

Aggressive braking after a brake job can cause overheating of the friction material, which brings the binders (glues) to the surface, known as glazing. This harder surface is prone to noise and can cause higher brake pedal effort until it wears away or is sanded to a flat surface. In many cases, the pads must be replaced when this happens.

Expected Brake Pad Life

It is difficult to predict just how long brake pads will last in terms of mileage or time because of varying driving habits and conditions. If a vehicle is used for towing or in constant stop-and-go traffic, the brakes generally require more frequent service. Younger drivers may go through pads more frequently due to last-minute stops. Some vehicles may require front brake service as much as three times more than rear brake service due to weight transfer and system design.

You may notice more brake dust on the front wheels than the rears when washing your vehicle. This is especially true on some European vehicles because many use more aggressive silicone-carbide brake pads resulting in more rotor wear and dark brown or black dust on the wheels. Some owners wax their wheels to minimize the dust formation.

If the front pads are severely worn or you find that they wear out frequently, be sure the rear brakes are working properly. Make sure the brakes aren't dragging due to a misadjusted pushrod in the master cylinder, too much fluid, or a misadjusted brake light switch at the brake pedal. Brake hoses with an internal restriction can cause the brakes to stay on, causing abnormal wear.

In rare cases, an ABS issue can contribute to excessive pad wear. For example, a mechanical problem within the ABS modulator on some vehicles can eliminate rear brake function and cause accelerated front pad wear.

Rotor Inspection

Be sure to examine the rotor surfaces for deep grooves and excessive wear. Some rotors have internal cooling fins and some are solid. Most front rotors have fins because they run hotter than the rear brakes. If your vehicle has a brake pulsation when stopping, you may have excessive rotor thickness variation (also called parallelism), which can develop due to lateral rotor runout. Machining or replacing the rotors is required to fix this issue.

You may also need to replace the rotors if they are badly worn or the thickness is below the minimum specification. A micrometer and dial indicator are required to properly measure your rotors for overall thickness and variation. The typical amount of runout allowed by many manufacturers is 0.003 inch, and thickness variation standards are even tighter at 0.0005 inch. As you can see, tolerances are pretty critical for proper brake operation.

Your local auto parts store should be able to measure the thickness and

If the pads are worn unevenly it could be an indication that the caliper or bracket needs attention. The slides could be binding or a pin or slider bolt could be seized. Further disassembly should reveal the culprit. A slight amount of normal uneven wear does occur on some systems due to caliper flexing.

A micrometer or dial caliper can measure the remaining rotor thickness to determine if it is still within the manufacturer's safety tolerance. A micrometer can also be used to measure the thickness at several locations to compare them and determine thickness variation (also known as rotor parallelism).

compare it to OEM specifications found in the vehicle service manual to make a recommendation as to whether the rotor can be machined or must be replaced. The service information often lists the nominal thickness, which is the thickness of the rotor when it was new. It also may list a "machine to" thickness. This is the minimum thickness that the rotor can be after it is turned on a lathe. If the rotor has deep grooves, measurements should be made at the deepest point.

If service information only lists a minimum thickness, the rotor is generally machined to about 0.030 inch larger so that it is still within tolerance after it "wears in."

You may also find specifications cast into the rotor or listed online. Be sure not to purchase poor-quality rotors if yours need replacement. Some shed iron particles that can embed in the new pads and cause noise. Impurities in the cast iron and improper heat treating during manufacturing are the common reasons for this. You don't want to have to do the job again in a couple of months.

If the rotors are within specification and you have no pedal pulsation or deep grooves, some manufacturers approve simple pad replacement only. This "pad slap" practice is often debated among professionals. Some shops have no problem with this approach while others machine or replace rotors on every brake job. One reason for this is that most shops do not possess a micrometer that can measure down to 0.0005 inch to determine if the thickness variation is within specification. They suggest replacement or machining to ensure that it is corrected if it is out of specification. Other shops feel that if brake pulsation does not exist when test driving, a pad slap is an option.

Another concern is that every time a rotor is machined, it has slightly less mass and therefore could run hotter during braking. Some professionals are concerned about the quality of the replacement and suggest that the machined OEM rotor with less mass is still better than some brand-new inferior replacements.

You also want to inspect the rotor surface for evidence of overheating and cracks. Bluing and hot spots can develop and are reasons to replace rather than machine.

A dial indicator can be used to determine the amount of rotor lateral runout. It is attached to the suspension system or caliper bracket and a dial gauge placed on the rotor surface. As the rotor is rotated slowly, runout causes the needle to deflect.

Rotor thickness specifications are available in the vehicle service manual and are also cast into the rotor in most cases. This specification is generally the minimum thickness, not the amount the rotor can be machined down to.

New or Rebuilt?

There seems to be the trend toward a throw-away world. Sometimes this is because the replacement part may cost less than repairing the old part. It is common with engines, starters, alternators, and even transmissions. Years ago, brake calipers, wheel cylinders, and even master cylinders were commonly rebuilt at a workshop. Most of these parts are now replaced with new when they fail due to the labor required and limited availability of parts.

Many shops replace rotors and drums rather than machine them. The choice is not always an easy one when faced with a grooved or pulsating rotor. Some shops feel that some replacements from overseas may be of lesser quality and choose to machine the originals, but others find that the price is close enough to the machining cost and have had success with replacements, so they go that route.

High-quality rotors and drums are available in the industry from name-brand manufacturers, but it is not always easy to tell if you are buying a quality piece. Just remember that as in many things, you get what you pay for, and doing the job over because a part failed might cost you much more in the long run. Quality components are especially important if your vehicle is used to haul heavy loads or pull a trailer. ■

On-Car Lathes

Lathes for machining rotors on the vehicle have been around for quite a while, but they are becoming more popular. Most shops have a lathe that can turn both rotors and drums, but the drums must be removed and taken to the lathe for machining. This means that the hub that the rotor or drum mounts to can still have some runout and cause the rotor or drum to have runout even though it may have been machined perfectly on the lathe.

That's where an on-car lathe is superior. It turns the rotor while mounted to the hub so that both assemblies are trued when the rotor is machined. The on-car lathe cannot machine drums, so they must either be removed for machining or replaced with new.

Caliper Inspection

One of the main areas to inspect the calipers are the slides or pins that the caliper must move on as the brakes are applied and released. As your vehicle ages, rust and corrosion can develop between the moving parts, creating issues. Calipers must be removed, surfaces properly lubricated, and parts replaced as necessary.

Binding slides cause uneven pad wear, possible noise, and inadequate braking. The pistons must be able to be pressed back into their bores if the calipers aren't going to be replaced to allow room for the installation of the new brake pads. The pistons are extended out of their bores because of pad wear; fluid had to take up that space behind the piston. This is also why the fluid level in the master cylinder drops as the pads wear.

Another reason that the fluid level drops is a leak in the system, but that would likely be accompanied by a sinking pedal, fluid on the ground, and a red brake warning light on the dash. Most of the time, the master cylinder is completely empty if a leak were present.

Service

Caution: Some newer vehicles with electronic brake systems require a scan tool for servicing.

(See "New Technology Precautions" at the end of this chapter before servicing a vehicle with an electronic brake system.)

Be sure to observe all safety precautions when performing brake service, including the use of wheel chocks, proper jack use and jack stands, safety glasses, ear protection, and disposable gloves. It is also wise to have good ventilation in the area and a fire extinguisher nearby.

Brake Fluid Condition

Brake fluid degrades over time. As fluid ages, it loses some of its additives. Although brake test strips are available to see if your fluid needs to be replaced, it's a good idea to replace it during brake servicing.

Although some manufacturers don't specifically recommend a replacement interval other than during hydraulic repair, it is a good

Brake fluid test strips are available to determine the condition of the fluid. They detect the level of copper present to determine fluid age and additive degradation. If the fluid is in need of replacement, the test strip turns purple within a minute of being immersed in the fluid.

Common Hand Tools Come in Handy

Most tools needed for disc brake repair can be found in the average do-it-yourselfer's toolbox. Bolts are generally metric in the range of 10 to 21 mm. Some vehicles use Torx or Allen-head fasteners. A torque wrench is needed to be sure all fasteners are safely tightened.

Tools for pushing back calipers are extremely handy but a C-clamp can be used against one of the old brake pads in most cases on the front. To push back rear caliper pistons that use integral parking brakes, a special tool that rotates the piston as it goes in is extremely useful.

If you are doing drum brake work, you need some inexpensive tools to remove and install hold-down and return springs. Tubing wrenches are the best for removing hydraulic fittings. A floor jack, jack stands, and wheel chocks are required for safe hoisting. ∎

A color chart is supplied with the test strips. After the strip is immersed in fluid from the master cylinder, it begins to change color if the fluid contains high levels of copper. If it becomes dark purple, a fluid change is needed.

check the vehicle manufacturer's specification. Put the cap back on the brake fluid bottle immediately because an open container absorbs moisture from the atmosphere and the fluid is ruined in a short time. It is also wise to buy small bottles of fluid for this reason.

Remember that brake fluid takes paint off quickly, so be careful where you place your hands after handling brake fluid and don't let any fluid drip on a painted surface. If it does, flush the surface with water immediately!

Brake Bleeder Removal

After you have raised and supported the vehicle, make sure the brake bleeders can be opened. This is necessary because the piston(s) in the caliper must be pressed back into its bore to allow room for the new, thicker brake pads. Also, the bleeder should be opened to allow potentially dirty fluid to escape instead

idea to begin the job by using a turkey baster to remove all of the old brake fluid from the master cylinder. Immediately fill the master cylinder to the maximum mark with the correct fluid and install the lid.

Most vehicles require DOT 3 brake fluid, but you should always

Test Strips Determine Amount of Copper

It is difficult to tell if brake fluid is bad by looking at the color of it. It naturally absorbs dye from the rubber components and turns darker as it ages, and most manufacturers don't have service intervals listed in the manual. A pretty common guideline is to replace the fluid every time the system is opened for service. A handful of manufacturers have a time interval, such as 24 months, but most do not specify a time or mileage interval.

Until recently, most professionals used a battery-powered device to determine the boiling point of the fluid, but now most are using test strips in the master cylinder reservoir. These strips determine the copper content of the fluid. The older the fluid, the more copper it has absorbed from the steel brake lines. This is an indication of age and additive degradation. The Society of Automotive Engineers (SAE) has determined that brake fluid with 200 ppm (parts per million) of copper or more should be replaced. ∎

Vacuum Bleeder Option

It is a good idea to first remove all of the old brake fluid from the master cylinder reservoir and pour in new fluid. This step keeps old fluid from entering the master cylinder and ABS unit when the system is opened up downstream. Brake vacuum bleeders are available for this purpose, but a common turkey baster works great if you have a container under the hood with you to squirt the old fluid into. Once the old fluid is out, you can pour in the correct fluid to the maximum line. The reservoir cap has the recommended fluid listed on it. ∎

Prior to beginning the brake job, it is a good idea to use a vacuum bleeder or turkey baster to remove the old fluid from the master cylinder reservoir. This prevents old fluid from flowing through the master cylinder and into the ABS modulator.

After the old fluid is removed, pour in new brake fluid until it is between the minimum and maximum mark on the master cylinder reservoir. When the calipers are removed or the bleeder is opened, new fluid circulates through the master cylinder and ABS modulator instead of old fluid.

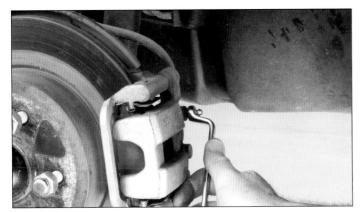

If the old calipers are to be reused, the bleeders must be checked to see if they open before starting the job. If they are unable to be opened without breakage, replacement calipers may be required. It is a good idea to open the bleeders prior to pushing back the caliper piston so that the old fluid can escape instead of flowing upstream through the ABS modulator and master cylinder.

If the bleeder is tight, try tightening it a bit first and then tapping it gently with a small hammer to free the rust around the threads. Do not use heat, which can cause internal damage to the caliper seals.

of traveling upstream. If a bleeder is stuck, lightly tap straight onto it with a ball-peen hammer and use a six-point wrench or socket. Tighten it a bit first and then loosen it. Tapping around the bleeder on the caliper can also help to loosen it. Do not use heat, which can damage internal rubber components.

Contamination and Precautions

Most vehicles today have ABS, and the hydraulic modulator that controls ABS operation is located between the wheels and the master cylinder. If the piston is pressed in without opening the bleeder, the fluid travels through the ABS unit on its way back to the master cylinder reservoir. This can allow dirt particles to clog passages in the ABS unit and ruin it. Some passages are smaller than the diameter of a human hair.

In the past, it was recommended to remove about half of the brake fluid from the master cylinder reservoir so that the fluid returning to the master cylinder as the pistons were pressed back could escape without overfilling the master cylinder reservoir. Most shops left the bleeder closed during a disc brake job.

This method does not take into account the potential of ABS unit or master cylinder internal contamination from dirty fluid in the calipers. The bleeder may be stuck from rust, which is why many people ignore this suggestion. You might be lucky, but it doesn't take much dirt to lodge in the ABS unit and create an expensive replacement. There is also a possibility of master cylinder damage from dirt particles.

As outlined earlier, it is good practice to completely remove all old fluid from the master cylinder with a turkey baster prior to repairs, fill it with new brake fluid, and open bleeders prior to pressing the pistons back. If new calipers are to be installed, it is still wise to remove old fluid and replace it with new so that the new calipers are not filled with old fluid when the brakes are bled. Don't clamp off the hose and then let dirty fluid into the replacement calipers after installation. Open the bleeders and let them drip into a pan until the new fluid makes it through.

At the end of the job, it is critical that you have the proper amount of fluid in the master cylinder reservoir. If it is overfilled, the fluid can expand as it heats up in the calipers and cause pressure in the system, even with your foot off the brake. This can cause the brakes to drag or lock on, damaging the new pads and rotors.

Brake Caliper Removal

Two common caliper attachment methods are used by most manufacturers. Some attach the caliper directly to the steering knuckle (part of the suspension system) and others have a bracket between the caliper and the knuckle. In either case, two bolts hold the caliper in position over the brake pads and two larger bolts hold the bracket to the knuckle (if equipped).

Many applications use bolts inside a bore encased in rubber or riding on O-rings with a special non-petroleum lubricant. This allows the caliper to slide as the brakes are applied and released. The pins or bolts are equipped with expandable boots to keep out contamination. The caliper is allowed to slide freely if the pins or bolts are clean and properly lubricated.

After the two bolts are removed, the caliper can be lifted off for pad replacement without removing the caliper bracket.

Most vehicles use two bolts to secure the caliper to the bracket or steering knuckle. Sometimes it is necessary to hold the sleeves that the bolts thread into to keep them from rotating as the bolts are removed.

Most vehicles have two larger bolts to attach the caliper bracket to the steering knuckle. These bolts (arrows) and the bracket must come off if the rotor is to be removed. They are prone to vibration and extreme heat cycling, so thread locker and proper torque are musts during reassembly.

After the bolts are removed, the caliper can be removed. If there is rotor wear or rust, a screwdriver or pry bar can be used to carefully pry the caliper off the rotor. If the piston must be pried back, use caution not to damage it.

If the caliper cannot be removed, there may be grooves in the rotor and the caliper piston may need to be pried back into its bore to allow caliper removal. Use extreme caution when prying the piston to avoid damage. Some calipers use phenolic pistons, which are very fragile. The caliper may also be corroded, causing difficult removal.

After removal, the caliper should be suspended by an S-hook or tied up with wire to relieve any stress on the brake hose.

Unless you are replacing the calipers, you can leave the calipers attached to the hose. Be sure to inspect the hoses carefully for cracks. The brake hose should never be clamped off during caliper replacement with locking pliers or even with a clamp designed for this purpose.

Tests have shown that the rigid liner inside the hose can crack, leading to hose restriction that can act as a one-way check valve in either direction. This causes the brakes to stay applied after a stop or may keep

fluid from flowing into the caliper, causing the car to pull to one side during braking. It is also likely that the hose will be damaged if the caliper weight is allowed to hang on it during service.

If the caliper is being replaced or removed, the hydraulic hose must be disconnected. Place a drain pan under the vehicle because fluid drips as the banjo bolt is removed. The fitting is called a banjo fitting because it resembles a banjo where the bolt goes through it. The fluid passes

When you remove the pads from the caliper or bracket, pay close attention to the position of the wear sensor (if equipped). The new pads should be placed in the same position.

The proper placement of the hardware and anti-rattle clips, guides, and shims is important. Be sure to mark their position or take a photo prior to removal. If any are omitted, clunking on braking or brake squeal is the likely result.

Don't let the caliper hang by the brake hose or ABS wires. An S-hook can be used so that the hose is not damaged. Be sure to position the caliper out of the way so that you can service the brakes easily.

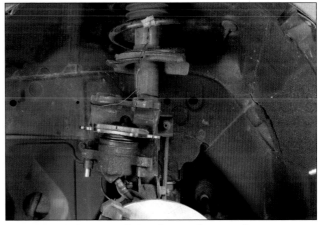

If you don't have an S-hook, use heavy wire to support the caliper. A good place to attach the caliper is the suspension spring or upper control arm.

Most brake hoses are attached to the caliper with a banjo fitting. A hollow bolt is sealed by two copper washers against a fitting that resembles a banjo. Proper torque is important so that it is leakproof without snapping the hollow bolt.

Don't Pinch the Brake Hose Flat

A common tire valve stem can be used to plug the banjo connection at the end of the brake hose where it attaches to the caliper. This prevents the master cylinder from going dry if you need to be away from the vehicle before you finish replacing the fluid. Be careful not to leave it too long because the valve stem may swell and become difficult to remove.

Many technicians pinch the hose flat with locking pliers or a special tool. Tests have shown that this damages the hose, so it should be avoided.

Top off the fluid in the master cylinder and pull out the valve stem so that clean fluid can enter and fill the system. Be sure to let the fluid drip into a pan you have placed under the hose. When you see clean fluid, you can attach the hose to the caliper. That way, you don't have old fluid in your new brake job. ∎

from the hose through a hole in the banjo fitting and through the hollow banjo bolt and into the caliper. The fluid fills the bore behind the piston with hydraulic pressure to move the piston into the pad and apply the brakes.

Allow the fluid to drip into the container until clean fluid is present. A common tire valve stem can be used to seal the banjo fitting if desired.

When reattaching the banjo fitting, use new copper washers. These are packaged with the replacement caliper and are also available separately or in an assortment pack at your local parts store. Make sure the hose is routed properly and not twisted before reassembly, and be sure to torque the banjo bolt correctly. It is hollow and can break if over torqued.

If the rotor is to be removed, the caliper bracket must be removed first.

The rotor surface should be extremely smooth so that the new pads have adequate surface

If you have to be away from the vehicle for a while, a good way to seal the banjo fitting prior to attachment to the caliper is to use a standard tire valve. This keeps the master cylinder from draining completely. Don't leave the valve stem in very long or it will swell and be impossible to remove.

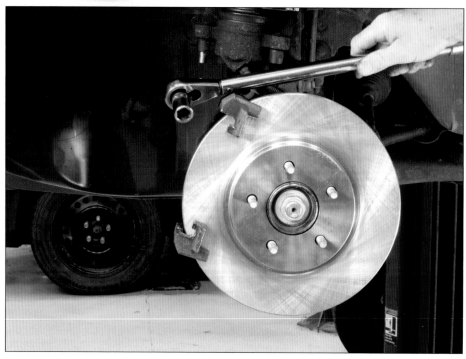

If the rotor is to be removed, the caliper bracket must be removed first. Two bolts secure the bracket to the steering knuckle. These bolts are generally pretty tight and often secured with thread-locking compound.

contact to perform without excessive pedal effort. After machining, some technicians add a non-directional finish to the rotor by using 125-grit sandpaper on a sanding block. They rub it back and forth as the rotor spins on the lathe for about 1 minute per side. This takes off the "peaks" or record groove effect (Remember records? They came before 8-track tapes!) and minimizes noise and excessive pedal effort by improving the surface contact between the fresh rotor surface and the pads. This process can help the pads more easily become "bedded in" or "burnished," which is discussed in detail at the end of this chapter.

After the rotors are machined, they should be washed with soap and water to remove all metal particles. This method works best and is less expensive than brake cleaner spray.

Rotors can be machined off the vehicle or on the vehicle with an on-car lathe. This method achieves optimal trueness by eliminating any runout that might exist between the rotor mounting flange and the hub

that it contacts. It must be smooth with the proper RA. A measurement device known as a surface profilometer is used. It has a stylus like an old-time record player that measures the surface as it is slowly moved across the face of the rotor.

Sometimes the cost of machining is close to the price of a replacement rotor, which causes many people to opt for new rotors. Just be careful that the rotor you are buying is of good quality. Poor-quality rotors generally develop runout and thickness variation issues more commonly than a

premium brand due to poor metallurgy. Rotors should be replaced in pairs to reduce the probability of a brake pull.

Rotor preparation is critical before installation. If the rotor was manufactured overseas, it likely has an oily or waxy coating. This must be removed prior to installation. Hot water and soap is by far the best cleaner after machining, but the coatings may not come off, so brake cleaner or some other solvent may be required. Don't clean the gray coating off German-built rotors. Install

Some vehicles are equipped with countersunk screws attaching the rotor or drum to the hub. Others may have stamped steel fasteners called Tinnerman nuts. These must be removed before the drum or rotor can be removed.

After the bolts are removed, the caliper bracket should slide off easily. Some applications have the pads mounted in the caliper bracket instead of the caliper itself. Do not mix up left- and right-side calipers or brackets. They can be accidently swapped on some applications.

The rotor can be removed on most applications after caliper bracket removal. If the rotor is stuck to the hub it is likely due to rust. If the flange is threaded, screws can be installed to assist in rotor removal.

If rust is a factor around the drum or the center pilot hole of the rotor, apply some penetrating oil and tap between the wheel studs with a hammer to loosen the bond. Some applications are prone to rust and can be difficult to remove.

An air hammer can be used to apply vibration to loosen the rust bond. Use a body-smoothing bit and apply vibration force between each wheel stud. Generally, a little patience and some penetrating oil will do the job.

them "as is." The gray coating is a "break-in" coat that conditions the new pads as they wear in.

If the caliper is to be reused, this is a good time to clean the slides and pins and lubricate them. Return the piston into the bore in preparation for the new pad installation. A C-clamp can be used against one of the old pads or a special tool can be used. There are several designs available. The piston must be pressed back completely to make room for the new brake pads. If a rear piston using a screw-type parking brake needs to be pressed back, a special tool is used so that the piston can be rotated on the actuator screw as it is pressed back. Electronic parking brakes may require special procedures.

The piston can be steel, aluminum, or phenolic. Phenolic is a synthetic material with superior heat resistance, but it can be damaged easily. Be sure to open the bleeder so that dirty fluid does not travel back upstream and damage the ABS unit.

If a replacement caliper is to be used, the piston is already in the

This "off-car" lathe can machine both rotors and drums. Various adapters are supplied with the lathe for different-size pilot holes and rotor diameters. A non-directional surface can also be made after machining using sandpaper or a rotary buffer.

The most effective way to clean a newly machined rotor or drum is to use soap and water. A scrub brush can loosen the metallic particles so that the water can flush them from the surface. This method is an industry standard and much less expensive than aerosol brake cleaners.

Be sure to clean the hub surface so that the new or newly machined rotor can fit properly. Check the lateral runout and reposition the rotor differently on the hub to achieve the least amount of runout. Install a wheel nut or two to hold the rotor onto the hub. This makes caliper installation much easier.

An "on-car" lathe is preferred by some vehicle manufacturers because it also takes into account any runout in the hub where the rotor mounts. On-car machining trues both the rotor and the hub, which eliminates brake pulsation.

Some rear disc brake systems use the pads for the parking brake. The parking brake is actuated by a cable, and a corkscrew type of drive screw extends the pads into the rotor when the parking brake is applied. This design requires a special tool that rotates the piston as it is pressed back into the caliper bore to make room for the new pads.

proper position for installation. A loaded caliper with or without a bracket is also available for most applications, which already has the pads installed. Replacement calipers are generally remanufactured, so look them over carefully prior to installation and be sure that all bolts are tightened to manufacturer's specifications and they don't have any significant wear points.

If you replace both sides, be careful to install them on the correct side of the vehicle. Some calipers can be installed vice versa so that the bleeders are on the bottom rather than the top, which prevents the air from being removed when you bleed the brakes.

Brake Pad Installation

When installing new pads, be sure that you place the pad with the wear indicator in the same position as the old one. Some pads are the same for the inner and outer position, but they often differ. It's easy to see the impression of the piston on the back of the old inboard pad,

so compare it to the new ones if you become confused. If the pads are inverted or the wear indicator is in the improper position, the pads may not seat in the caliper correctly and cause poor braking performance or contact with the wheel as it rotates.

Make sure the slides and pins or bolts are cleaned and properly lubed. The slides and pins can be lubricated with silicone brake grease or caliper lube provided that is not petroleum

One method for pushing a normal caliper piston back into its bore is to use a common C-clamp against one of the old brake pads. Open the bleeder first to keep old fluid from entering the ABS modulator.

based. Don't use anti-seize compound or regular chassis or wheel bearing grease because it causes the rubber parts to swell and bind the calipers.

When installing the new pads into the calipers or brackets, avoid touching the friction surface. A good idea is to use painter's tape on the friction surface and remove it right before installing the pad against the rotor. Be sure that the new hardware and shims are in the proper position.

Special tools are also available for pushing the piston back in the bore. Some C-clamps are difficult to use on two-piston calipers, making the special tool very helpful. Avoid using groove-joint pliers, especially on phenolic pistons due to the possibility of piston breakage.

Some late-model vehicles using a caliper bracket require bolt replacement each time the bracket is removed. (Check the service information for your vehicle.) These are torque-to-yield bolts similar to engine cylinder-head bolts. Most vehicles have reuseable bolts. In either case, be sure to apply thread-lock compound and torque them to proper specifications.

Be sure to apply the proper lubricant to the moving parts so that the brakes give you long, trouble-free service. Do not use any petroleum-based lubricants or anti-seize on rubber brake parts because they will swell and bind. Silicone brake lubricant is a good choice for the rubber parts (not RTV sealer).

Brake Caliper Installation

After the slides are cleaned and lubed and the hardware replaced and lubed, install the rotor (if removed) and hold it in place by installing a few lug nuts. Install the caliper bracket, apply thread locker to the bolts and torque them to factory specification.

Some newer vehicles require bolt replacement because they are torque-to-yield. Install the pads onto the bracket or into the caliper and slide the caliper over the rotor and into its mounting area.

Be careful not to twist the brake hose during installation. A twist shortens the hose and may cause it to pull apart during a sharp turn. Lubricate the pins or bolts and install them per the manufacturer's guidelines. Do not lube the threads. Attach any anti-rattle clips.

Open the bleeders and allow them to gravity bleed into a suitable container. Note that some vehicles don't always gravity bleed. Foot bleed or vacuum bleed and then pump the brakes lightly until the pedal becomes high and hard. Do not press the pedal to the floor; use half-pedal

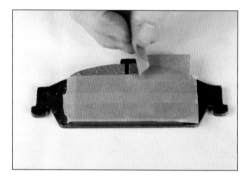

A layer of painter's tape on the friction surface of the pads keeps dirt and fingerprints off until you are ready for final assembly. This is also helpful for brake shoes on drum brake systems.

As the caliper lines up with the attaching bolts, be sure the sliders are in the proper position. Some have flats that must line up with a ledge at the edge of the caliper. Others may have wrench flats that must be held with an open-end wrench while the two caliper bolts are torqued.

After final assembly, open the bleeders with drain pans under them for a gravity bleed. Afterward, foot or vacuum bleed until the fluid is clean and free of bubbles at each wheel (see chapter 6: Hydraulic Brake Systems for more information about brake system bleeding).

Pump the pedal with the engine off to cause the pads to seat against the rotors. The pedal should be high and hard and unable to be pumped after the initial seating. Forgetting this step can result in an accident because the first pedal application may go to the floor before the pads seat against rotors.

This step is important because it tests for hydraulic leaks. Have an assistant start the vehicle and pump up the pedal and then hold firm force on the pedal. With a flashlight, examine the entire brake system, especially where you had the system open. Pay particular attention to the banjo fittings at the calipers.

movements instead to avoid damaging the master cylinder.

This ensures that the pads are seated against the rotors. Many shop accidents take place because someone forgot to "pump up the brakes" after a brake job. The vehicle is backed into a parked or passing vehicle because the first few pedal strokes do nothing since the pads are not seated against the rotors.

Start the vehicle and have an assistant press hard on the brakes while you check for leaks at the wheels and at the lines, hoses, and fittings. Pay particular attention to the banjo fittings. The hydraulic lines on some applications are prone to rust, so look carefully at the metal lines, especially around brackets.

Break in the Brakes

When a brake job is completed, the friction material and rotor and drum surfaces are not completely smooth or mated with each other. The first few miles of driving after a new brake job are very important. The way the brakes are applied can help the two relatively rough surfaces smooth out and conform to each other. This is known as "breaking in" or "burnishing" the pads. It is also known as "bedding in" the pads. As this happens, the surface contact area increases and the brakes require less pedal effort to stop the vehicle.

The rotor finish is extremely important. The smoother it is, the better. Brake engineers measure a surface with a surface profilometer. It can assign a number rating to a surface in RA. Some brake manufacturers recommend an RA of 14-70 on a rotor surface.

For reference, a piece of glass is about 4 RA. It is not possible to machine a rotor to that level of smoothness with a common lathe or to purchase one that smooth. You wouldn't want that anyway because some amount of pad material transfers to the rotor on initial braking, which helps the break-in process.

A minute amount of roughness is a good thing, but many rotors are very rough when the new pads first touch them. This causes high pedal effort to stop the vehicle, excessive brake dusting, and possible brake noise from the vibration caused by the low surface contact. The pads are actually sitting on mountain peaks that must be worn down before the brakes perform as they should. Heavy braking with the pads in this condition can cause overheating and actually bring the adhesives inside the pad to the surface. This is called glazing and can contribute to more noise.

To reduce this potential, purchase or machine the rotors to a smooth surface and then drive the vehicle using a procedure that burnishes the new friction material properly. ∎

Test Drive and Break-In

When brake materials are new, they should be broken in just as with a brand-new engine. In brake terminology, this is called burnishing or bedding in the pads. Vehicle manufacturers follow a specified FMVSS break-in procedure for new vehicles that requires 200 special stops or slow-downs. This would be difficult to do in a shop environment or your neighborhood due to the time required. As an alternative, 20–25 stops from 30 mph or slow-downs from 50–30 mph with a time of cool down between each stop is more practical.

Here's the procedure. Find a large, empty section of a parking lot where you can drive alone and take time to do it right. Apply light to medium pressure on the brake pedal to a stop from about 20–30 mph and then wait 30 seconds or so for the brakes to cool down. Repeat this 20–25 times and avoid heavy braking during this process.

You can also make a few stops in reverse to be sure the rear drum brakes (if equipped) are adjusting properly. This procedure breaks in the new friction material and smooths the rotor or drum so that better surface contact is obtained.

For the first few days of use with the new brakes, try to avoid aggressive stopping. In time, the two surfaces become almost like mirrors and achieve nearly 100-percent surface contact to provide the best possible braking.

New Technology Precautions

Some newer applications with electronic brake systems may require the system to be placed in service mode with a factory scan tool prior to brake service. This is to eliminate the possibly of the system performing a self-test during the brake job. Pressures can be as high as 2,000 psi in the electronic brake system and more than 400 psi at the wheels during the self-test. Refer to your vehicle's service information prior to servicing the vehicle and refer to any published technical service bulletins (TSBs) related to your vehicle.

If your vehicle is equipped with electronic parking brakes, a scan tool may be needed to retract the rear caliper pistons prior to the installation of new brake pads.

Many newer vehicles are equipped with electronic brake systems. A scan tool may be necessary to put the vehicle in service mode prior to working on it for safety purposes. Another use of the scan tool besides diagnosis is to retract the rear caliper pistons prior to pad replacement.

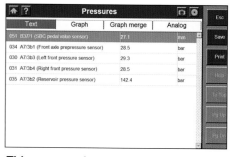

This scan tool screen capture illustrates the extreme hydraulic pressures found in some vehicles with electronic brake systems. In the Mercedes Sensatronic system, you can have 400 psi at the wheels and more than 2,000 psi in the modulator. It is for this reason that the service information should be consulted before beginning any brake service. A scan tool may be required to disable the system during brake service.

A break-in procedure ensures that the new friction material seats correctly to the rotors and drums. Aggressive stopping should be avoided if possible. The longer the test ride, the more the two surfaces can seat to each other and improve braking ability.

DRUM BRAKE SYSTEMS

Caution 1: The information in this chapter is based on general knowledge and may not be specific to your vehicle. Specific information is available in the factory service manual for your vehicle, which should be consulted for torque specifications, procedures, and safety.

Caution 2: Some newer vehicles with electronic brake systems require a scan tool for servicing. See "New Technology Precautions" at the end of this chapter before servicing a vehicle with an electronic brake system.

Although many vehicles have four-wheel disc brakes, your vehicle might be equipped with a drum brake system on the rear axle. Drum brakes were the first brake systems used on early vehicles. The first designs used a friction band around the outside of a drum that the wheel bolted to. Most vehicles had them only on the rear.

When the brake pedal was applied, a long metal rod from the brake pedal moved a lever that squeezed the band around the

Drum brakes today use hydraulic systems that are effective and reliable. The master cylinder forces fluid through lines and hoses to all four wheels and stopping ability is far superior to the systems of old. Drum brakes were once found on all four wheels, but disc brakes have replaced them in the front and many vehicles also have disc brakes in the rear. This particular design uses a single-loop spring that acts as both the hold-down and return springs.

spinning drum, hopefully bringing the car to a halt. No hydraulics were used and this design was also subject to water contamination and rust because it was exposed to the elements. Brake pedal kickback also occurred when the vehicle hit bumps due to the axle pushing and pulling on the metal rod. Vehicles were heavy

and some were capable of 60 mph, so stopping was difficult at best. This type of band is used inside some automatic transmissions today.

Operation

Today's internal shoe drum brake systems have many advantages

A Moog Tidbit

I once spoke to the Moog family of Moog Automotive in St. Louis about their 1919 Buick, which has the early drum brake system. Mr. Moog stated that the vehicle would "go like heck," but stopping it was another matter. He went on to say that it would stop eventually, but you might have to use the guy in front of you. ■

The brake drum is over the internal shoes so that they are better protected from the elements, but water can still enter during heavy rain. The drum also retains a good bit of heat, so the internal components are subject to heat-related damage. The drum slides over the wheel studs so that it is directly connected to the wheel. When the brakes apply, the wheel is slowed, which slows the vehicle.

This drum from a 1952 Ford F2 truck is a unicast design. This means that the hub is part of the drum assembly and has serviceable wheel bearings. To remove this style of drum, the grease cap is removed to access a cotter pin and castle nut. After the castle nut is removed, the outer wheel bearing is removed, then the drum. This design is sometimes found on the rear wheels of front-wheel-drive vehicles also.

over that old Buick, but the modern drum brake system hasn't changed much since its invention in the 1930s. Two brake shoes are forced against the inside of a spinning drum when the brake pedal is applied.

Mounted between the shoes is a wheel cylinder that contains two pistons. Hydraulic pressure from the master cylinder moves them into the shoes. Hold-down springs keep the shoes in position and return springs pull them away from the drum after the pedal is released. Most drum brake systems use a backing plate with three support pads behind each shoe. These pads have a thin layer of lubricant for the shoes to slide on as they apply and release. The friction material wears down as the brakes are used, requiring adjustment to maintain pedal height.

After the wheel is removed, the drum slides off the wheel studs. On older models, the hub may be part of the drum and a nut and outer wheel

Inside the drum are two brake shoes that expand when the wheel cylinder pistons move outward under pressure. The fluid pressure comes from the master cylinder when the pedal is applied. Return springs retract the shoes when the pedal is released. Hold-down springs keep the shoes in the correct position on the backing plate.

The drum is made of cast iron and has cooling fins on the outside and a machined drum surface on the inside. Some drums are known as composites, which means that they use a steel plate cast into the mold to provide less weight than a full cast drum. Some drums were also aluminum composite on older vehicles.

Early drum brake vehicles did not have self-adjusters. The brake shoes had to be adjusted periodically to account for shoe wear or a low brake pedal resulted. This 1952 Ford front brake has only one piston applying the brakes (arrow). The shoe it actuates presses into the spinning drum, which transfers energy to the other shoe, which wedges into the drum. This is called servo action.

Manual brake adjustment is accomplished by a tool called a brake spoon that is inserted through a slot in the backing plate or drum. The spoon can turn the star wheel teeth to expand the brake shoes inside the drum. On older vehicles without automatic adjusters, a spring is in contact with teeth so that they cannot turn after the adjustment is made. When the brakes are adjusted properly, pedal position is correct and the brakes do not drag. Modern drum brakes can be manually adjusted too.

Modern vehicles with drum brakes have automatic adjustment. The star wheel is turned automatically by an internal lever. It can also be manually adjusted with a brake spoon.

Many vehicles with rear disc brakes now use a miniature drum brake system inside of the rotor for the parking brake. It is applied by a cable from the parking brake lever or pedal and can also be applied by an electric motor on vehicles with electric parking brakes. These brakes also use a star wheel on many applications that must be adjusted properly for adequate parking brake operation. Because the parking brake is only on when the vehicle is stopped, adjustment is not commonly needed.

The automatic adjuster system consists of a cable or rod that moves a lever against the teeth of the star wheel, rotating the star wheel. This causes the adjuster to expand on its threads to adjust the shoes closer to the drum. The star wheel teeth are only turned if the distance between the brake shoes and drum is excessive.

bearing must be removed prior to removing the drum.

Older drum brake systems did not have automatic adjustment and sometimes had only one piston in the wheel cylinder to actuate one shoe. The spinning drum caused that shoe to transfer force to the other shoe and wedge the brake shoe into the drum to stop the vehicle.

Modern brake systems have mechanical automatic adjusters to maintain proper operation and brake pedal height as the brake shoe friction material wears away. A threaded mechanism known as a star wheel expands to spread the shoes if an excessive gap is present between the shoes and the drum. The star wheel has teeth that are turned by a ratcheting lever through a cable or rod that moves if adjustment is required. Some brakes auto-adjust when the brakes are released in reverse; others adjust when the parking brake is used.

Drum brake systems have one feature that disc brakes do not have. They are able to self-energize and use servo action to increase braking ability by wedging the brake shoes into the spinning drum. For this reason, the force required to apply them is minimal compared to disc brakes, which must be clamped to the rotor with high pressure to stop.

Drum brakes do a better job than disc brakes when they are used as parking brakes. Many modern vehicles with four-wheel disc brakes have a small drum brake system inside the rear rotors for parking brake operation.

Wheel Cylinder Operation

The wheel cylinder contains cup seals and pistons that extend when the brake pedal is applied, pushing the shoes into the drums to stop the vehicle. Older models used a residual check valve in the master cylinder to maintain a low pressure inside the system to hold the cup seals in position, but this has been replaced with an internal spring between the cups inside of each wheel cylinder. A dust seal is used on each end of the wheel cylinder to protect the unit from contamination. Most vehicles have only one wheel cylinder at the top, but a few vehicles have two wheel cylinders per wheel.

Even though all drum brake systems have a wheel cylinder, a shoe anchor, shoes, springs, adjusters,

The wheel cylinder contains two pistons that push the brake shoes into the rotating brake drum to slow or stop the vehicle. It is bolted or held to the backing plate with a retaining clip. The brake line attaches to the back of it to supply the pressurized fluid from the master cylinder. Older vehicles have cast-iron wheel cylinders but most drum brake vehicles today have aluminum wheel cylinders.

This is a cutaway of a typical wheel cylinder showing the internal components. There are a variety of bore sizes depending on the weight, size, and the intended purpose of the vehicle. The internal spring maintains force on the two wheel cylinder cups to keep them against the pistons.

The internal components of a common wheel cylinder include two pistons, two cup seals, two dust seals, and a coil spring. Fluid under pressure between the cup seals moves the pistons outward. The brake shoes are pushed into the drum by the moving pistons as they expand.

and a drum, there are actually two different types of drum brake systems: self-energizing and leading/trailing.

Self-Energizing Drum Brake Systems

The self-energizing or duo-servo design uses a shoe anchor at the top, a star wheel at the bottom, and two different-length shoes. It is used on older vehicles and some light trucks, SUVs, and vans when more stopping power is required. The rear shoe is longer. When the brakes are applied on this type of system, one shoe applies force to the other through the star wheel adjuster, wedging it into the drum. The wheel cylinder may apply the initial force, but it really just starts the wedging action as the drum spins.

Some tractor brakes use the same approach but do not have hydraulics and apply mechanically.

Self-energizing brakes work in both forward and reverse, but in forward mode, the shorter front (primary) shoe applies force to the longer (secondary) shoe, which is most effective.

Leading/Trailing Drum Brake Systems

Most modern lightweight vehicles with rear drum brakes use a leading/trailing system. Unlike the self-energizing/duo-servo type, the shoe anchor is at the bottom and the adjuster is at the top. Each shoe can function independently. There is wedging action into the drum with each separate shoe, but one shoe does not increase the force of the other shoe, so the stopping power of this system is not as powerful as the duo-servo type.

Both shoes are the same length and sometimes they even have the same part number. In this design, the front shoe is referred to as the leading shoe and does most of the work when going forward. The rear shoe is the trailing shoe and does most of the stopping when backing up.

If you remove a drum and see the anchor at the bottom and the same amount of friction material on each shoe, you are looking at a leading/trailing system. If you see the anchor at the top and a longer rear shoe, you have a self-energizing/duo-servo design.

A duo-servo or self-energizing drum brake system uses brake shoes with different lengths of friction material attached to the shoes. The rear shoe has a longer length of material and does most of the work when stopping forward motion. When the wheel cylinder expands, this shoe is wedged into the drum by the rotation of the drum causing the front shoe to apply force into it through the star wheel. This is how it got the name self-energizing. Oddly enough, the shoe doing the bulk of the stopping is called the secondary shoe (longer shoe) and the other is called the primary shoe (shorter shoe). The anchor point that the shoes contact is at the top. This is the easy way to tell if your vehicle is a duo-servo design.

The most common type of drum brake system in use today is called leading/trailing. Both shoes are the same length and sometimes even have the same part number. They both receive the same apply force from the wheel cylinder and have no self-energizing between the shoes because they work independently of each other. The anchor point is at the bottom on this design. Leading/trailing systems do not have as much force as duo-servo designs.

System Inspection

Because the friction material on brake shoes wear as they are used, they need replacement at some point. This varies due to driving habits and vehicle type, but they usually last much longer than the front disc brakes. In some cases, they may last as much as three times as long due to the fact that most of the vehicle weight is up front and the weight transfers forward when braking. On some vehicles, as much as 90 percent of the braking is handled by the front brakes.

Many light-duty pickup trucks with drum brakes rarely need shoe replacement unless they are contaminated by brake fluid or gear oil. This occurs pretty frequently on some domestic applications.

Brake shoes must always be replaced if contaminated since the liquid soaks into the friction material like a sponge. Cleaning them with brake spray is not recommended because it cannot fully remove liquids that have soaked into the friction material. Contaminated shoes lock up when applied because the fluid cooks into a sticky mess when heat is applied during braking. Of course, the axle seal or wheel cylinder that caused the contamination must also be replaced or it will ruin the new shoes.

Shoe Inspection

There are obviously other reasons that brake shoes may require replacement besides fluid contamination. Badly cracked or damaged linings or linings worn below the safety standard also need to be replaced. The state you live in may have a vehicle safety inspection program that has a specified tolerance for brake lining thickness and component inspection. Often a bonded lining has a minimum thickness of 1/16 inch and a riveted lining of 1/8 inch (or 1/16 inch above the rivet head).

You may choose to replace your shoes before they wear to this point for preventative maintenance and

The friction surface on a brake shoe wears down as the brakes are applied. Routine inspection helps to ensure that the friction material does not completely wear away, causing damage to the drum and reduced braking. This shoe was totally ignored, which undoubtedly caused audible noise and performance issues before it completely failed.

Brake shoes may also be damaged by fluid contamination from the wheel cylinder or axle seal. No matter the cause, contaminated shoes should be replaced and not cleaned. Contrary to what might be expected, contaminated brake shoes often cause the brakes to grab when applied because the fluid heats up and becomes sticky. Here the axle seal is being replaced before installing new brake shoes so that the problem does not reoccur.

You can see the axle seal around the axle shaft on this pickup truck. It is not leaking. If an axle seal is found to be leaking, be sure that the axle is not severely worn prior to replacing the seal. Excessive up-and-down movement due to a bad wheel bearing or worn axle shaft will cause a new seal to leak. Also be sure that the differential vent hose is clear of mud and debris. Pressure build-up inside of the housing can also cause a seal to leak.

Severely cracked brake shoes should be replaced. If the cracks are a result of excess heat or smell burnt, you may want to find out how the vehicle is used. Severe-duty friction material might be available for the application to upgrade it for heavier use. Inspect the drum to make sure it was not damaged by the cracked shoe.

The friction material has separated from the riveted brake shoe on this old brake system. Replacement is required. The wheel cylinder has also leaked onto the shoe and contaminated the brake system with brake fluid, causing the brake dust to cling to the surfaces instead of exiting the drum.

better stopping. You can consult service information for your vehicle to obtain the actual specifications. You can measure the thickness of the material remaining with a multi-colored gauge or a steel tape measure. Special measuring tools are available to measure the amount of friction material remaining above a rivet head or you can use spring-loaded and digital caliper tools for obtaining precise measurements.

Brake-thickness gauges are available to measure the amount of friction material remaining on brake shoes and pads. Some give an indication with visible colors to make a determination. Red is the thinnest gauge, which means that immediate service is needed. Yellow means that service is needed soon. Green indicates that the linings are still within specifications.

Most vehicle manufacturers and many states that have mandatory vehicle safety inspection programs have standards for how thin the brake linings on a shoe can be. Some specify as little as 1/16 inch on bonded linings. If the linings are attached with rivets, measurements are taken in the rivet hole with the most wear around it.

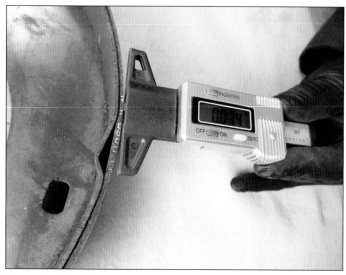

Some brake-thickness gauges precisely measure the lining thickness. After the thickness reading is obtained, the amount left can be compared to the specifications in the service manual to determine if they are within manufacturer or state inspection specifications.

Many vehicles have an inspection hole with a rubber plug (arrow) that can be removed to view the thickness of the remaining brake shoe material without removing the drum. Although this is helpful, the drum should be removed to get a proper look at the entire system. It is possible for the shoe to have more wear in a spot that the inspection hole does not reveal.

Drum Inspection

Check the drum for grooves, tapered or bell-mouthed wear, hot spots, cracks, and proper diameter. If the linings have worn down too far, the metal part of the shoe can make contact with the brake drum and cause damage, which requires the drum to be machined or replaced. Hot spots and serious cracks are caused by excessive heat and require drum replacement. Small grooves are the result of dirt between the drum and brake shoes. The drum may be able to be machined if the damage is not severe. If the drum is badly damaged or worn beyond maximum diameter specifications, it requires replacement.

Cost may dictate which way you decide to go because the cost to machine a drum may be close to the price of a new drum. Just be sure the drum you purchase is of good quality. This is one area where you get what you pay for.

Special tools are available to measure the diameter of the drum to determine if it can be machined or requires replacement. The specifications are available in the service information for your vehicle, or your parts store can look up the specifications for you and machine the drums if needed. The maximum-diameter specification may also be visible on the drum itself because the law requires it to be cast into the metal.

As brakes are used, the lining material wears, and the drum wears a small amount also. If the friction material wears completely off the shoe, the metal framework comes in contact with the drum and causes damage. To determine if a drum is still within specification or if it still has enough material left to be machined, a drum micrometer is used. It reads the inside diameter of the drum in inches or millimeters. Some are mechanical and some newer models are digital. After machining away the grooves, the drum is re-measured; if it is over the specification, it must be replaced.

This drum was damaged from metal-to-metal contact with the shoe after the friction material had worn away completely. Periodic inspection helps to eliminate this type of damage. Failure to recognize or ignoring brake noise may also lead to the need to replace the drum, which results in higher costs during service.

A brake lathe uses a bit to machine away a small layer of iron inside the drum. It trues the surface and removes grooves and other imperfections. If the grooves are deep enough that machining them away makes the diameter larger than the "machine to" specification, the drum must be discarded. Usually, the cost of the labor to machine a drum is less than the cost of a new drum, but if the costs are close and the new drum is of good quality, some technicians recommend new drums because the increased mass reduces the heat and the potential for noise.

You may come across a "machine to" tolerance and a "maximum diameter" tolerance. There is usually about 0.030 inch between the two to allow for break-in of the drum surface after machining. In other words, the drum must not be machined down to the maximum diameter because it will be out of specification after "wear in" occurs.

Always machine both sides to maintain similar diameters or replace both sides. This eliminates the possibility of a brake pull after you finish the job due to different diameters causing different levels of brake force on each side.

Backing Plate Inspection

If the shoes are worn unevenly or one shoe is worn significantly more than the other, several other components should be inspected. The backing plate where the shoes ride contains six support plates on most vehicles. These may have developed grooves, causing the shoes to catch when they are applied or released. This is usually the cause of a popping noise from drum brakes. If the backing plate is damaged, some have welded and refinished the

The backing plate holds the brake shoes in place inside the drum. There are three raised shoe support pads on the backing plate (arrow shows one of the support pads). When the brakes are applied, the shoe slides on the pads and they return to their normal position when the brakes are released. It is important that the pads have no deep grooves and are lubricated so that the shoes can move freely. Deep grooves can cause the shoes to catch when applied or released, causing a popping noise.

If the shoe support pads are badly worn, the backing plate should be replaced. Many applications have a replacement available that can be installed without axle removal after cutting off the old plate. A separate piece bolts in after installation that fills in the hole at the bottom.

surface, but replacement of the backing plate is recommended. Some have a bolt-on portion at the bottom so that they can be installed after cutting away the old one. This is so you don't have to remove the axle if replacement is required.

Hardware and Adjuster Inspection

Another cause of uneven wear could be worn, rusted, or fatigued hold-down or return springs (known as brake hardware). It is a good practice to replace the hardware during a brake job because a visual inspection may not reveal problems caused by excess heat. A kit is available with everything you need for both sides. It is referred to as a combi-kit.

If you need parts related to the brake adjusters, they are available in a kit for the right side or the left side and are stamped with an "L" or an "R." These are referred to as adjuster kits. The kits contain the star wheel, cable or arm, and related springs and retainers. Be careful to install the correct star wheel on the correct side or the brakes will not adjust properly and the brake pedal becomes lower as the shoes wear. The auto adjuster components should be inspected to ensure proper operation.

The star wheel threads must turn freely and the teeth must not be worn or corroded. The cable or lever and spring must be properly assembled so that the movement causes the lever against the star wheel to adjust it when necessary. A common mistake is to assemble the auto adjuster components improperly, resulting in a low brake pedal over time because the star wheel is not extending as the brake shoes wear.

Wheel Cylinder Inspection

A binding or sluggish wheel cylinder piston can also cause one shoe to wear more than the other. Check the wheel cylinder pistons to be sure that they move freely by pushing in on each piston. The wheel cylinder should be replaced if a pis-

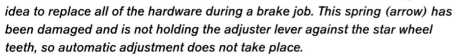

If any brake hardware is damaged or a spring is stretched, badly rusted, or has wear from contact with other components, replacement is required. Heat damage is not always visible, so it is a good idea to replace all of the hardware during a brake job. This spring (arrow) has been damaged and is not holding the adjuster lever against the star wheel teeth, so automatic adjustment does not take place.

This star wheel had severe rust that kept it from turning when the adjuster lever contacted it. The vehicle had a lower than normal brake pedal. After replacement and proper adjustment, the pedal height was restored. Be sure that the components are properly assembled. A small mistake can prevent the adjuster from working properly and affect pedal height and brake performance. Star wheels have opposite threads on left and right sides, so do not mix them up!

The star wheel is responsible for adjusting the shoes closer to the drum as wear occurs. If the star wheel is binding from rust on the threads or the teeth are damaged, the brakes do not adjust properly and the brake pedal becomes lower than normal. Be sure to inspect the star wheel and clean and lubricate the threads and the pivot points during service. Also check the corresponding cable or lever and springs. If replacement is needed, a left- or right-side adjuster kit can be purchased that contains the star wheel and all necessary hardware.

ton is stuck, leaking, or binding. If the brake fluid leaks around the cup seals and pistons, it drips from the dust boots, down the backing plate, and onto the drum and shoes.

Also inspect for leaks by gently pressing on the dust boots or lifting the edge. This action could rip the dust boot, so be very careful. A small amount of seepage may be present, but excessive fluid loss in the form of droplets means that the wheel cylinder should be replaced. Some manufacturers do not recommend lifting the edges of the dust seal for fear of damaging it.

In the past, many shops honed out the bore of the wheel cylinder and rebuilt it with new cup seals and dust boots, but most now replace the entire unit to save time and reduce the potential for a reoccurring failure. Many late-model aluminum wheel cylinders are not designed to be rebuilt because the internal surface is compromised if a ball hone is used. If one side is leaking, it is good practice to replace both sides since they were likely subjected to the same conditions.

Remember that new brake shoes have thicker friction material, so if the old wheel cylinders are reused, the pistons have to be pressed in as you reassemble. If you install new drums that have a smaller diameter than the worn drums, the pistons go in even farther! This could cause the seals to push through internal sludge that builds up over the years and cause piston binding or cup leakage. It just makes sense to replace the wheel cylinders during drum brake service.

Parking Brake Inspection

Accelerated or uneven shoe wear can also occur due to the parking brake system binding or left on during driving. In areas of harsh winters with heavily salted roads, the parking brake cables tend to rust internally and bind, keeping the brake shoes partially applied even though the parking brake lever or pedal is released. Be sure that the cables are free and the shoes fully retract when the parking brake is released.

Although it may be possible to apply penetrating oil to the outer casing of the cable, binding cables require replacement because many

To determine if a wheel cylinder is leaking past the piston cup seals, many technicians slightly lift one edge of the dust boot or press on the dust boot to see if brake fluid drips out. Be careful not to damage the dust boot during the inspection process. Some manufacturers allow a very small amount of fluid between the cup seal and the dust boot but not to the point of fluid running out when the boot is pressed or the edge lifted. Some shops choose not to lift the boot due to possibly damaging it. If the boot emits fluid when pressing on it with your finger, the wheel cylinder is leaking.

If a wheel cylinder is found to be leaking, replacement is required. The leaking fluid ends up on the brake shoes and inside the drum. Aluminum wheel cylinders are not meant to be rebuilt. Most technicians replace them because they are fairly inexpensive and the possibility of internal pitting of the bore. It is also becoming difficult to find internal parts.

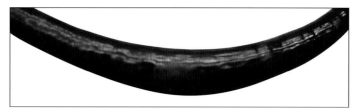

A rusted brake cable can cause the brakes to stay on or drag. Most brake cables now have a plastic outer shield to resist rust intrusion, but water can get under the shield. Swelled areas in the shield indicate internal rust. If there is no plastic outer shield, it might be possible to spray the outside with penetrating oil and work the cable free, but it usually binds up again down the road. In areas of high salt use, the cables often fray at the ends and break. If you find a rusted brake cable, replacement is required.

Before beginning drum brake service, the brake dust needs to be washed away so that you do not breathe it in. In most professional shops, a "bird bath" sink is used for this purpose. It uses a water-based solvent and filter bag to remove and trap the dust. In the past, brake dust was high in asbestos. Even though the levels were reduced, it is still not safe to breathe brake dust and an air blowgun must never be used to clean the system.

now have a plastic outer layer. If you see a bubble or swelled portion under the plastic outer layer, it is an indication of internal rust, which can restrict the movement of the inner cable, hindering brake release and causing brake drag.

In the home garage, many use aerosol brake cleaner spray with a drip pan underneath for the purpose of cleaning the drum brake components. Be careful not to breathe the vapors in a closed garage and wear gloves if your hands are sensitive to solvents.

System Service

The first step when drum brake service is required is to remove excess dust inside the drum so that it is not inhaled during service. You should *never* use a blowgun and shop air to blow off the dust of a brake system. Special equipment is available for this purpose that uses a water-based liquid to prevent the dust from being inhaled and causing serious respiratory problems. This is a requirement in some states at professional auto repair facilities.

Asbestos has been banned for use in other industries and it has been greatly reduced in automotive brakes, but it has not been totally eliminated, so caution is very important. Some experts wear a dust mask to limit the intake of brake dust when servicing brakes.

You may be able to use a garden hose to wash down the dust before and after drum removal, but this may not comply with local regulations in your area due to runoff. Another option is to use a drain pan and aerosol brake cleaner spray. You can spray some cleaner between the backing plate and the drum prior to drum removal and then spray down the components after drum removal, allowing the cleaner to drip into the pan below. The spray is highly evaporative and leaves solids in the drip pan.

Drum Removal

Some drums are held to the axle or hub flange by small Phillips or Torx screws that must be removed prior to drum removal. These must be reinstalled after service to ensure that the drum is properly centered. Some

drums also have threaded holes to allow bolts to be installed, which act as pullers to remove a rusted drum.

Other drums use retainers over the wheel studs called Tinnerman nuts. These are not designed to be reused. You can remove a Tinnerman nut with side cutters by grabbing one of the internal nibs near the stud threads and twisting it to break the nut. These are only needed during vehicle assembly to keep the drums from falling off on the production line. The wheel holds the drum in place when the lug nuts are installed.

A few applications use a drum attached to the hub by pressed wheel studs and these drums do not slide off. The wheel bearing cap, cotter pin, and bearing retaining nut must be removed first. When sliding the assembly off the spindle, be careful not to allow the outer wheel bearing to fall to the floor. Some applications, such as Hyundai and Kia, use a staked nut that must be replaced with a new one.

On one-ton trucks, the rear drum has the drive axle bolted to the drum with eight bolts. These must be removed and the axle pulled from the axle tube to gain access to the wheel bearing retainer and adjusting nut. Some one-ton trucks use a slide-off rear drum, but most do not.

On slide-on designs, it may be difficult to remove the drum from the vehicle. Rust can develop on the flange around the center pilot hole or the wheel studs. It can also develop between the vertical surface of the hub and the drum. Use a hammer to tap or air hammer to rattle on the drum between the wheel studs and around the center pilot hole. You can also tap around the drum edge

but not to the point of damaging the drum. Some penetrating oil may be applied around the center pilot

and studs to help dissolve the bond, but be sure to clean it off before reassembly.

The rust bond around the center pilot hole or between the drum and hub can be broken loose by tapping on the drum. Do not use heavy force to avoid damage to the drum and be careful not to hit the wheel studs. Penetrating oil can be used but must be removed afterward to keep it off the brake components.

An air hammer is also effective when a brake drum is stuck on due to heavy rust buildup. Use a flat-body smoothing bit and vibrate it between the wheel studs to loosen the rust bond between the flange and around the center pilot hole. You can gently use it around the outer diameter, but use caution so that you do not damage the drum.

Some drums have threaded holes to allow bolts to be installed, which act as pullers to remove a rusted drum. Others are centered by tapered Phillips- or Torx-head screws, which must be removed prior to removing the drum. If they are stuck, a brass drift can be used to tap directly on them. This jars the threads and allows removal. Be sure to install them after the job.

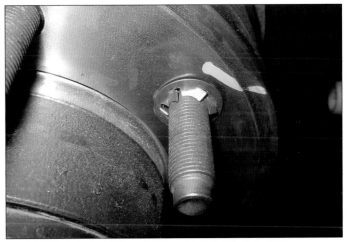

Tinnerman nuts are sometimes used to retain the drums or rotors on the assembly line. On full-frame vehicles, the frame is usually upside down during undercarriage assembly and is then rolled over prior to installing the vehicle body. Tinnerman nuts must be removed prior to drum removal. They are not designed to be reused, so they can be broken off with side-cutting pliers and discarded. The wheels hold the drums on after the Tinnerman nuts are removed.

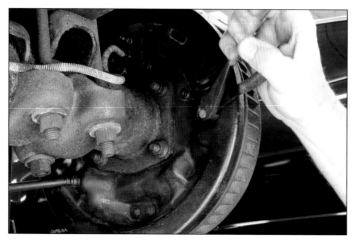

If the brake shoes are wedged into grooves inside the drum and the star wheel cannot be adjusted to back off the shoes to remove the drum, another option is to cut the heads off the hold-down pins with side cutters or a similar tool. This allows the shoes and hardware to come off as the drum is removed. Then you can reach inside the drum and disassemble the components piece by piece.

The brake bleeder screw (arrow) is located on the wheel cylinder on the inside of the backing plate and must be free to turn so that the brakes can be bled after the brake job is complete. The wrench flats on the bleeder screw usually accept an 8- or 10-mm wrench. Be sure to use a six-point bleeder wrench or a six-point socket so that it does not slip and round off the flats on the bleeder screw. Try to tighten it a little first. This can sometimes help to break the rust free without damage to the bleeder screw.

Another reason that the drum may be difficult to remove is that the shoes may be grooved and caught on corresponding grooves inside of the drum. It may be possible to adjust the star wheel to back the shoes away from the drum through the adjustment slot in the backing plate or drum. A slim screwdriver can be used to hold the adjuster lever away from the star wheel teeth so that it can be backed off. If the shoes cannot be backed off, you can cut off the hold-down pin heads on the backside of the backing plate and pull the entire assembly from the vehicle while still inside the drum. Of course, you need new pins and they are included in the hardware kit.

Brake Bleeder

If you haven't already done so, be sure the brake bleeder can be loosened without breaking. Several methods can be used if the bleeder is badly rusted or tight. If a bleeder is stuck, *lightly* tap straight onto it with a ball-peen hammer and use a six-point wrench or socket. Try to tighten it a bit first and then loosen it. Avoid heat, which can damage internal rubber components.

Return Spring Removal

It is important to take a photo of each side before removal for reference. Place a towel or paper towels on a cart or bench so that you can lay the parts down in position as they are removed. Another method is to leave one side together so that you have a reference in addition to your photo. Of course this is all based on whether or not previous service was done correctly. If you have any concerns about proper component location, consult factory service information for your vehicle.

If the bleeder doesn't turn easily, don't force it. Be patient and you might be able to remove it instead of breaking it off. Try tapping gently on the bleeder with a small hammer. This action tends to break the threads loose from the rust. Penetrating oil can be used to help soak into threads to free them from the rust. Some technicians use a small amount of heat from a torch or an electric induction heater. The concern here is damage to the rubber seals inside the wheel cylinder.

It is a wise idea to take photos of the drum brake system prior to disassembly. Some of the spring and lever attachments are quite complex and a photo can come in handy during reassembly, provided the person who serviced the brakes before you did it right! Another option is to leave the other side of the vehicle together and use it a reference, but remember that some of the components will be backward on the other side. Spread out a towel and lay each part on it in the same position it was on the vehicle.

After cleaning the assembly with the appropriate method, most technicians remove the shoe return springs first. Pliers can be used to accomplish this, but a brake spring tool works much better. Place the round part of the tool with the pin on it over the anchor pin. Rotate the tool so that it hooks under the spring and then tilt the tool downward to pop the spring off the anchor pin. Do this to both return springs and then remove them and lay on a shop towel in the location they were on the vehicle.

Many service methods can be used, but the one in your vehicle's service information is likely the most effective. Although brake shoe designs and hardware vary from vehicle to vehicle, generally the brake return springs are removed first. A special and inexpensive universal spring tool is available for this purpose. It is much more effective than pliers or side cutters and does not damage the springs if used correctly. Place the end of the tool over the shoe anchor and position the pin under the spring. As you rotate the tool, angle it slightly; the spring should come loose easily.

Lay the spring on the towel in the position it was on the vehicle. Now remove the return spring on the other shoe and lay it in position. The auto adjuster lever or cable may also be retained by a return spring or a hold-down spring and attached to the anchor. You can next remove the

After the return springs are removed, you can spread the shoes apart slightly and remove the parking brake strut between the shoes. Pay attention to the position of the spring on the strut. Proper reassembly is critical to parking brake operation. Also, if any parts are installed incorrectly, they can become loose and fall into the drum to be badly damaged as the drum spins.

parking brake strut (spreader) being careful to keep the pressure spring in the proper position. If it has a hooked end, pay attention to its location.

Hold-Down Removal

The shoe retaining springs (also called hold-down springs) can be removed next. They use pins with flattened tips that install through a spring and flat retainer clip. An inexpensive special tool is available for removal and installation of the shoe retainers. You reach around the backing plate with one finger and hold the pin against the plate as you press in on the retainer and compress the spring. Next, turn the retainer a fourth of a turn (90 degrees). The retainer should now be free of the pin, allowing the spring to release.

Auto Adjuster and Parking Brake Lever Removal

The shoe may still be partially retained by springs on the bottom and possibly by the parking brake lever attachment. Be careful not to drop the star wheel adjuster or lever. Remove the spring at the bottom and the star wheel and place them on the towel in the position they were on the vehicle. Repeat the process on the other shoe, paying attention to the position of each component. One shoe is attached to the parking brake lever or cable. It may be necessary to pry open a retainer or remove a snap-ring to remove the lever from the shoe. Lay everything on the towel in the position it was on the vehicle.

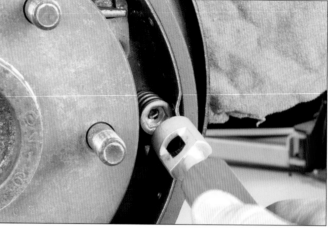

After the return springs and parking brake strut are removed, you can remove the shoe retainers and brake shoes. Pliers could be used here, but a special tool designed for this purpose is available at a reasonable price. Position the tool over the shoe retainer and, while holding the back of the hold-down pin, push in and compress the spring while turning the tool a quarter turn.

After removing one shoe retainer spring and pin, remove the corresponding spring and pin on the other side. Inspect the retainers carefully. They might be functional, but it is a good idea to replace the hardware during a complete brake job.

The star wheel and associated components should be easy to remove from the brake shoes. Lay each component on a shop towel or tabletop in the same position as it was on the vehicle. This makes reinstallation much easier.

It might be necessary to disconnect the parking brake cable lever from the brake shoe. Some applications use a horseshoe-shaped washer that must be bent open; others use an E-clip that is simply pried off. A few applications use a groove in the shoe for the parking brake cable lever with no retainer.

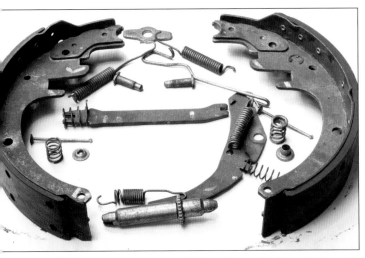

After all the parts are removed from the vehicle and placed on a towel or cart, it is much easier to inspect them for wear or damage. If some of the parts are to be reused, this is a good time to clean them thoroughly. Use brake cleaner spray and a bristle brush.

Most wheel cylinders are attached to the backing plate with two bolts that have 10-mm heads. Removal and replacement is pretty straightforward, but be sure to start the metal hydraulic line nut by hand before tightening the bolts. This allows some movement so that you do not cross-thread the line. After the bolts are tightened, use a flare-nut wrench to tighten the line nut.

Wheel Cylinder Replacement

If the wheel cylinder needs to be replaced, do it now. It may use push-rods coming out of the dust boots that can be removed prior to wheel cylinder removal from the backing plate. On some applications, it is helpful to remove the bleeder screw to gain more access to the brake line attachment nut. Use a flare nut wrench so you don't round off the nut. The wheel cylinder is usually attached to the backing plate with two 10-mm head bolts. Some GM applications use a spring retainer, which can be more difficult to remove and install.

If the nut is rusted to the line, turning it twists the line and ruins it, so use caution. A slight amount of heat from a propane or butane torch can be used to help free the nut from the line, but overdoing it damages the internal components of the wheel cylinder, requiring replacement. Remember that brake fluid on your fingers damages painted surfaces and that brake fluid burns when it is exposed to a flame.

Some wheel cylinders are secured with a metal ring instead of bolts. This is generally found on GM vehicles. The ring is more difficult to deal with than bolts. To remove the wheel cylinder, the ring must be pried off, which usually damages it. Be sure to wear safety glasses! The new wheel cylinder comes with a new retaining ring.

The wheel cylinder retaining ring can be installed using a 1⅛-inch 12-point deep socket and a common C-clamp. Position the wheel cylinder through the backing plate and place the ring on the backside of the plate. Using the C-clamp and socket, press the ring until it snaps into the retaining ledges on the wheel cylinder.

Be Careful When Removing the Wheel Cylinder

On the GM spring clip design, the new wheel cylinder comes with a new retainer, so don't worry about ruining the old one as you remove it. However, be sure to wear safety glasses and be careful because it can fly off during removal. Install the new retainer with a 1⅛-inch socket and a C-clamp against the wheel cylinder. ∎

If the brake line nut has rusted to the tubing, you might be able to remove the bolts securing the wheel cylinder and unscrew the entire wheel cylinder from the line. After the wheel cylinder is no longer connected to the line, you can heat the nut on the line to free it up before reassembly without damaging the wheel cylinder from excess heat.

Keep an eye on the master cylinder reservoir fluid level during service. Do not let it go empty because it is extremely time consuming to remove air out from the ABS unit and lines. Top off the fluid from time to time during the brake job to eliminate this possibility and keep the lid on to reduce moisture intrusion.

Another option if the line nut is rusted to the line is to remove the wheel cylinder attachment bolts and carefully flex the brake line enough to pull the wheel cylinder away from the backing plate. Hold the nut with a flare nut wrench and unscrew the wheel cylinder from the nut. After removal you can heat the nut and quench it with some cold water to break it free of the line. Use caution because brake fluid can ignite when heated.

Parts Installation

After it is removed, cap off the line with a rubber cap or a short length of hose with a screw in the other end so you don't lose all the fluid in the master cylinder. Always keep a close eye on the fluid level of the master cylinder during the brake job so that it does not go dry. Air in the system can be difficult to remove, especially if it gets into the ABS unit.

When installing the new wheel cylinder, line up the brake line first and tighten it by hand before installing the retaining bolts. This allows you to insert the line into the port without cross threading it. After the line nut is started, you can tighten the two retaining bolts and then finish tightening the line nut. Cross threading the nut may cause damage that requires another new wheel cylinder and a new line. Reinstall the bleeder screw and tighten if it was removed.

Backing Plate Preparation

Thoroughly clean the backing plate and lubricate the six shoe

Before installing the new parts on the backing plate, be sure to thoroughly clean it and lubricate the six shoe support pads. Apply a thin layer of brake lubricant so that the shoes can move freely as they are applied and released. If the pads are badly worn, the backing plate should be replaced.

support pads with the proper lubricant being careful not to use too much. Excess lubricant can get onto the shoes and into the drum and affect braking. You can use special brake lubricant here or even anti-seize compound, but do not use common wheel bearing grease because it will melt and run onto the shoes due to the heat that develops inside the drum during normal braking.

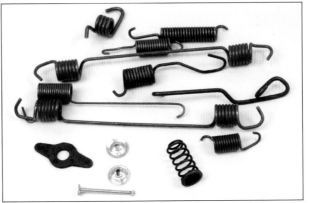

A brake hardware kit (or combi-kit) contains everything you need to install the new shoes except for the auto-adjuster parts. These are sold separately as a right- or left-side kit. All retainers and return springs are included in the hardware kit.

Shoe Installation

Brake shoes are sold in axle sets with four shoes, two for each side, in the box. Some are identical but many have a longer lining on two shoes or a parking brake lever attached to two shoes and have a left and a right shoe. Remove the new brake linings from the box and completely cover the friction surfaces with masking tape so that you do not get dirty fingerprints on the linings during installation.

Save the box in case you are required to return the old shoes as cores. This is becoming less of a requirement, but some suppliers still rebuild shoes.

Hardware Installation

Open the new hardware kit package and verify that all springs and components match the originals. Place the shoe retaining pins (they resemble nails) through the backing plate toward you and lay the springs, retainers, and retainer tool within reach.

Hold-Down Installation

Attach the parking brake lever to the appropriate shoe and place it in position on the backing plate. Refer to your photo or the other side to be sure you are installing the correct shoe in the proper position. Remember that if one shoe has longer friction material, it is always installed toward the rear and usually is the one the parking brake lever attaches to. Using the retainer tool, compress the spring with the retainer and turn the tool a quarter of a turn (90 degrees) as you hold the pin against the backing plate. On some applications, the parking brake cable guide and lever goes under one of the retainer springs.

Repeat the process on the other shoe and align the wheel cylinder pushrods into the shoes (if equipped). Install the parking brake strut (spreader bar) with the tension spring in the proper position between the two shoes.

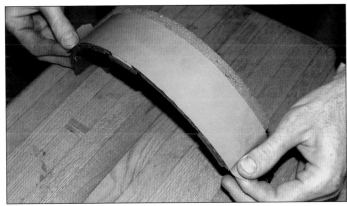

Before you begin installation of the new brake shoes, one option is to cover the friction surfaces with masking tape. This keeps them clean during the process. After the shoes and all other components are installed, remove the masking tape just before installing the brake drum. This is not a necessary step but can help keep things clean.

To install the brake shoe hold-downs, place the pin through the backing plate from the back side and install the shoe. Place the spring and retainer in position and compress the spring with the special tool while twisting it 90 degrees. Be sure the pin is properly engaged with the retainer.

Place the parking brake strut between the brake shoes with the spring in the proper position. Make sure that the forked ends are properly aligned and the parking brake lever contacts the strut. Improper positioning can affect parking brake operation and cause parts to fall into the drum.

Use the special spring tool to install the other return spring. Using pliers for this purpose can be difficult and can damage the spring. Be sure that the looped end of the spring was not stretched open during installation. The spring can be squeezed slightly with pliers to close up the loop if this has occurred.

Auto Adjuster and Return Spring Installation

Install the auto-adjuster lever or cable and guide and then install the two return springs with the special tool. It works similar to a shoehorn. Place the spring over the end of the tool and use the tool to guide the spring onto the anchor by lifting it. The spring slides down the tool and pops into place.

In most cases, it is easier to install the lower retaining spring and then pull the shoes apart to install the star wheel after it has been adjusted to its shortest width. Be sure that the spring is not upside down and rubbing on the star wheel teeth. This prevents proper adjustment when driving and the brake pedal eventually becomes lower.

After all parts are installed and checked for accuracy, be sure that the auto adjuster works properly when you pull the cable or move the lever. Be sure to remove the masking tape before installing the drum.

Drum Installation

Install the machined or new drum in the proper position so that the tapered retaining screw can be installed (if equipped). Be careful not to touch the friction surface on the shoes or drum with dirty hands. If this happens, you can use some brake cleaner or denatured alcohol on a rag to wipe the fingerprints away, but do not saturate the new shoes.

Adjustment

You need to adjust the star wheel so that the shoes are close to the drum surface but not to the point that the drum is excessively difficult to turn after installation.

A special tool is available to gauge the diameter of the drum and

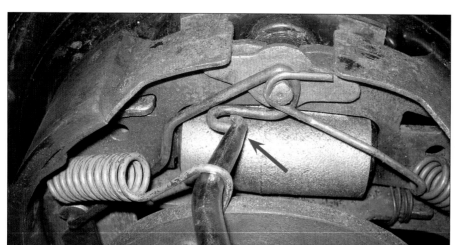

A brake spring tool should be used to install the shoe return springs. Place the open end of the spring over the tool and position the tip of the tool over the anchor pin or auto-adjusting link (arrow). Lift the tool and the spring will slide into position on the anchor pin.

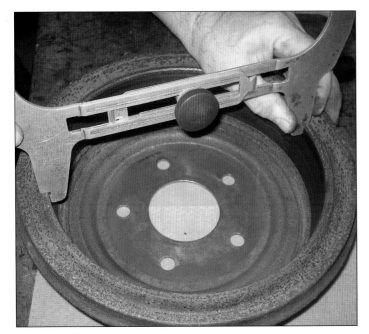

If a shoe gauge adjustment tool is available, it can be placed inside the drum as a guide to adjust the brake shoes. A lock nut holds the tool in position after gauging it to the inner drum diameter.

The other side of the gauging tool is placed over the two shoes and they are adjusted by turning the star wheel by hand until the shoes contact the tool. This sets the shoe adjustment close to the final setting. It is still important to recheck the adjustment after the drum is installed and the shoes are centered by applying the brake pedal. A little more adjustment is generally required.

set the shoes to that diameter. It is placed inside the drum and opened up until the ears are against the inside friction surface. A lock nut holds it in position. The other side of the tool is that same dimension and the shoes are adjusted until they contact the surface of the gauge.

Adjust the star wheel so that the shoes expand; then, slip fit the drum over the shoes until you cannot rock it when it is about halfway on. This means that the adjustment is pretty close, but because the shoes can move somewhat on the backing plate, there is no guarantee that they are properly centered until the drum is installed and the brakes have been applied. Doing this centers the shoes inside the drum and the final adjustment can be made afterward.

To ensure proper brake pedal height, you need to make a final adjustment through the adjustment hole in the backing

When the drum is installed over the new shoes, it should just slip over them and slightly drag as the drum is rotated. This is a judgement call and takes a little practice. If the adjustment is too loose, the brake pedal will be lower than desired. If the shoes are too tight, the brakes drag and could overheat.

plate or drum until there is a slight drag on the drum when turning it. The closer the shoes are to the drum, the better the brake pedal height, but adjusting the shoes too tight causes them to drag and

damage the new friction and possibly the drum from heat. Repeat the process on the other side and then bleed the brakes. Refer to chapter 6: Hydraulic Brake Systems for bleeding suggestions.

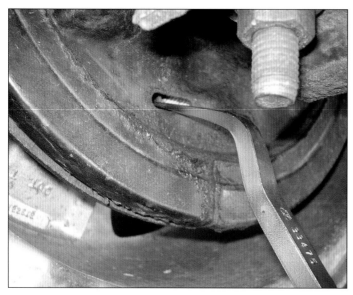

After the drum is installed and the shoes are centered by stepping on the brake pedal, the final adjustment can be achieved by using a brake spoon to turn the star wheel through a hole in the backing plate or brake drum. Be careful not to adjust the new brakes too tight, but if they are too loose, the brake pedal is abnormally low.

Test drive the vehicle to make sure it stops correctly and does not pull to either side during braking. Be sure that the brake pedal height is correct. Burnish (break in) the new friction material to the drum surface by performing a number of light to normal stops with cool-down time between each stop. Avoid panic stops. A large, empty parking lot works well to avoid traffic. Apply the brakes when backing up to allow additional adjustment to take place. After the test drive, recheck the fluid level in the master cylinder reservoir, but do not overfill it.

After bleeding is completed, start the vehicle and pressure test all hydraulic connections and the new wheel cylinders for leaks. If self-energizing brakes are adjusted too loose, they can lock up as the primary shoes jumps to engage the secondary.

Test Drive and Break-In

After installation of the wheels and properly torquing the lug nuts or bolts, the vehicle needs to be test driven and the new friction material properly bedded in or burnished (seated to the drum surface).

The key is to stop several times with light to moderate pressure from about 30 mph with a cool-down period between each stop. Try not to stop aggressively as in a panic stop because damage can occur to the new friction from excess heat. Be sure to back up the vehicle and apply the brakes and the parking brakes to ensure that they auto adjust properly. After driving several conservative miles, it is a good idea to recheck the torque on the wheels and recheck the fluid level in the master cylinder reservoir.

New Technology Precautions

Prior to any brake service, consult the factory service information. Some systems can perform a self-test unexpectedly, which could pressurize the system and lead to injury if the system is being serviced. A scan tool may be required to put the system in "service mode." This mode keeps the electronic module from pressurizing the system until repairs are completed.

On late-model vehicles, extremely high brake pressure can occur at any time due to a system self-test, potentially resulting in personal injury. Check the factory service information to determine if the system needs to be disabled prior to a brake job. This scan tool capture shows pressures in excess of 2,000 psi in a Mercedes system.

Pressures				
Text	Graph	Graph merge	Analog	
051 B37/1 (SBC pedal value sensor)		27.1	mm	
034 A7/3b1 (Front axle prepressure sensor)		28.5	bar	
030 A7/3b3 (Left front pressure sensor)		29.3	bar	
031 A7/3b4 (Right front pressure sensor)		28.5	bar	
035 A7/3b2 (Reservoir pressure sensor)		142.4	bar	

Esc | Save | Print | Help

PARKING BRAKE SYSTEMS

For many decades, vehicles have been equipped with a parking brake system. It is separate from the vehicle's base brake system.

Operation

When the vehicle is parked, the parking brakes are applied either mechanically with cables through a lever or pedal or electrically with a switch. Some can even apply automatically. The parking brake helps the transmission hold the vehicle in place when at rest.

In the event of brake failure, the parking brake system may provide some braking, but it cannot provide the same level of braking as the vehicle's base (main) brake system. For this reason, many manufacturers do not use the term "emergency brake" for the system. "Parking brake" has become the industry standard name for the system. Early parking brakes sometimes applied a brake band around a drum attached to the driveshaft. A lever inside the vehicle actuated the band.

On modern vehicles, the system consists of a cable-actuated mechanism to apply part of the base brakes or a separate friction component on the rear wheels. Some newer vehicles incorporate a small electric motor in the rear calipers or a motorized cable system to apply the pads when the vehicle is stopped. The motorized cable can also be used with

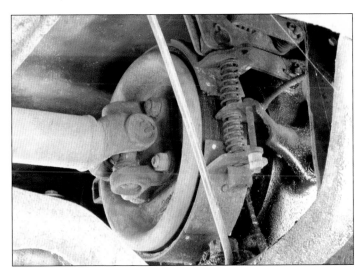

A parking brake system is used in addition to the vehicle's base brake system. This is an early parking brake from a Ford truck, which holds the driveshaft instead of the rear wheels. It uses an external band brake to squeeze around a drum attached to the driveshaft.

On a modern vehicle, the parking brake is usually applied by a lever or pedal inside the vehicle. This vehicle uses a lever in the center console. The parking brake is usually mechanically applied using cables (arrows) instead of using hydraulics as the base brakes do. Some later models use an electric motor to apply the system manually or automatically.

Vehicles with rear drum brakes use the base brake drum system for the parking brake function. Drum brakes perform better than disc brakes when used for parking because of their self-energizing action. If the drum attempts to rotate, the shoes wedge harder into the drum, making them even more effective.

A commonly used parking brake system on vehicles with rear disc brakes is referred to as "drum-in-hat." This name comes from the fact that a small brake drum is cast into the "hat" section of the rotor. The drum system is only used when the parking brakes are applied, so the friction material has little or no wear because the vehicle is stationary.

drum-type parking brakes. There may be a dash-mounted switch or the system can apply automatically when the vehicle is shifted into Park or one of the doors is opened. Some use small brake shoes inside a drum, which is cast into the rear brake rotors. This rotor is referred to as a "drum-in-hat" design.

The parking brake friction material should not wear like the base brakes do because they only apply when the vehicle is stopped. On some vehicles, it is easy to accidently drive the vehicle with the parking brake on, which could cause excessive wear to the friction material and damage to the system from overheating. Most vehicles have a red brake warning lamp (RBWL) and/or an audible warning when the vehicle is moved with the parking brake applied.

A vehicle equipped with rear drum brakes likely uses a cable to apply the parking brake and a brake strut or spreader bar between the two brake shoes. The parking brake

lever or pedal pulls the cable, which uses an offset lever inside the drum to press one shoe (usually the rear shoe) into the drum. The moving lever is in contact with the brake strut, which applies the other shoe.

Generally, drum parking brake systems work well because they use the self-energizing, wedging effect of the shoes into the drums. It is more difficult for disc brakes to perform this function.

When the parking brake is applied, most vehicles illuminate the red brake warning lamp (RBWL) to alert the driver that the parking brake is applied. This reduces the possibility of driving with the brake on. This lamp can also illuminate when the fluid level is low or a hydraulic system leak is present.

A conventional drum brake vehicle uses the same brake components as the base brakes do, but the shoes are applied by a lever mechanically rather than using the wheel cylinder. A brake strut between the two shoes transfers the force to the other shoe when the parking brake is applied.

Some rear disc brake systems do not use an internal brake shoe system for the parking brake. A corkscrew type of mechanism inside the caliper pushes the caliper piston out to squeeze the pads against the rotor. It can be cable or motor actuated. When replacing the rear brake pads, the piston may need to be rotated to fully seat it and make room to accept the new, thicker pads.

A vehicle equipped with rear disc brakes may use a cable or motor to squeeze the brake pads in the caliper against the rotor when parked. This can be done automatically or mechanically with a lever or pedal. The apply force is accomplished by a drive screw that functions like a corkscrew to apply the pads. Because disc brake systems do not have self-energizing action like drum systems, they often do not work as well as drum-type parking brakes.

Inspection and Service

On all applications using a cable, some amount of cable stretching may occur over time, requiring adjustment. Some models have threaded adjusters in the center of the cable and others adjust at the pedal or lever connection.

It is not uncommon for cables to become severely rusted, leading to problems in harsh climates. Many cables have an outer plastic shield.

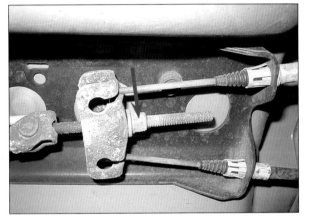

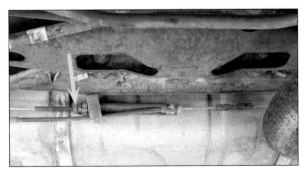

It may be necessary to adjust the tension on the cables if the cables stretch over time or new cables are installed (arrow to adjusting nut). When applied, the parking brake should be able to hold the vehicle, but be sure not to adjust them too tightly or the brakes will drag during driving.

Here is another style of cable adjustment (arrow to adjusting nut). Because these are under the vehicle, they are often contaminated with dirt or rust. Apply some penetrating oil before attempting to adjust the nut.

If that shield appears to be bloated or swelled, the cable is internally rusted. Some of the most common problems are cable lockup due to internal rust. This often causes the brakes to remain applied after the lever or pedal is released or drag when driving. Another result of rust

---

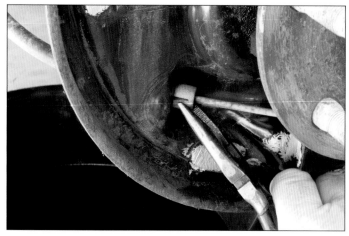

The outer parking brake cable housing is attached to the backing plate with metal "fingers" that expand when the cable is inserted. They must be compressed to allow removal of the cable from the backing plate. Sometimes needle-nosed pliers can accomplish this.

If pliers do not compress the fingers adequately, the outer housing can be disconnected from the backing plate using a small hose clamp. Open the clamp, place it around the cable attachment "fingers," and then tighten the clamp until they are compressed enough to allow the cable to be removed.

In most cases, the inner parking brake cable attaches to a lever inside the drum. If the cable must be replaced, the end has a ball that must be disconnected by compressing the spring enough to allow it to drop out of the lever. Needle-nosed or side-cutter pliers are useful here.

A small box-end wrench can also be used to press the cable attachment fingers for removal. The most common size is 13 mm. The fingers on the new cable do not need to be compressed. Just push the cable into the hole in the backing plate and the fingers pop out into place.

is a cable that is severed and cannot function at all. In both cases, the cable must be replaced. Most cables are available from the aftermarket and are not generally difficult to replace. Be sure to wear safety glasses when under the vehicle.

To replace a cable, the inner cable end must be disconnected from the lever that attaches it to the brake shoes inside the drum. A spring makes this a bit of a challenge, but in most cases, the spring can be "inched back" with needle-nosed or side-cutter pliers, allowing the end to be released.

Most cable housings are snapped into the brake backing plate using metal "fingers" that snap open when installed. To release these retainers, the fingers must be compressed. A pair of needle-nosed pliers might do the job, but if the fingers cannot be easily compressed, place a hose clamp or box-end wrench around the fingers to compress them. This presses them in and allows you to pull the cable housing from backing plate. You need to disconnect the inner cable from the parking brake lever to allow removal.

The other end of the cable is attached to a second cable that leads to the pedal or lever in the vehicle. Spray some penetrating oil on it before attempting to remove it. Be careful because the old cable is often frayed and sharp.

The drum-in-hat design uses a rotor that has an internal drum cast into it. Some models use two brake shoes that resemble a normal drum brake system. Sometimes you find that the rear axle seals on rear-wheel-drive vehicles have leaked gear lube onto the internal parking brake shoes, requiring replacement.

The other end of the cable is likely connected to another cable leading to the lever or pedal in the vehicle. It will be rusty, so apply some penetrating oil before attempting to disconnect it. Be careful around frayed cable to avoid injury.

Drum-in-Hat Parking Brakes

Some vehicles with rear disc brakes use a small drum brake system inside the rear rotors for the parking brake. Some applications have two shoes with springs and an adjuster just like conventional drum brakes, but they do not self-adjust. General Motors uses a one-piece shoe on many applications.

These are called "drum-in-hat" systems and they can be applied with a cable or an electric motor controlled by a switch or automatically when the vehicle is parked. Drum-in-hat designs generally perform better than the cork-screw caliper system because they self-energize.

This one-piece parking brake shoe is common to GM vehicles and does not use return springs. The horseshoe-shaped unit flexes when the parking brake is applied. It is held to the backing plate by small retainers that can sometimes rust away and allow the one-piece shoe to spin around inside the drum, causing damage.

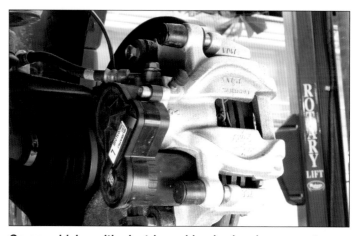

This is a drum-in-hat rotor. If the drum surface is damaged, it cannot be machined because it reduces the structural integrity with the rotor face. Damage or severe rust requires rotor replacement.

The electric motor that retracts the cable on an electric parking brake (EPB) system often uses a rack-drive gear-set for the required torque, but the teeth are sometimes made of plastic, which can wear. The unit may contain strain gauges to electrically determine the amount of force that the brakes are receiving.

Electrically Applied Parking Brakes

A trend on newer vehicles is toward electrically applied parking brakes. Some use a dash-mounted switch and some activate automatically when the vehicle is parked or one of the doors are opened. A strain gauge may be used by the parking brake module to detect the amount of stretch in the cable.

This determines how much force the motor should apply. Some models monitor the amperage increase in the motor to determine force. The latest designs monitor ABS wheel sensors and increase brake force when parked if movement is detected. These designs provide less effort since a parking brake pedal or lever is no longer required, but there are some drawbacks.

Many late-model vehicles are equipped with electrically applied parking brakes. Some use a switch on the instrument panel and others are automatically applied when the vehicle is placed into Park or a door is opened. Some models monitor the ABS sensors and, if movement takes place, they apply the brakes harder.

Some vehicles with electric parking brakes have a motor inside each rear caliper with a gear or belt to apply the piston, which presses the pads against the rotor. This design almost always has a special method to retract the piston when the pads require replacement. Servicing electric parking brakes can require the use of a scan tool.

The components are more costly and the system is generally either on or off, so it cannot be used to apply variable force when driving to safety after a brake system failure.

The apply motor might also be built into the rear calipers instead of being cable driven. This causes an increase in cost if the calipers need replacement.

You also may need special electronic tools or a factory scan tool to retract the rear caliper pistons for new pad installation during a rear brake job. Some models have a "work around" to service the rear brakes without a scan tool. Consult your vehicle's owner's manual or service manual.

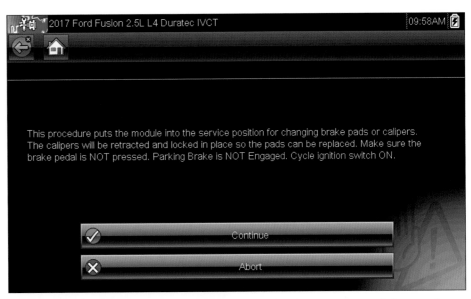

Many models with electrically applied parking brakes use a special procedure to retract the caliper piston if the pads need to be replaced. This vehicle is being prepared for rear pad installation with a scan tool.

This electric parking brake (EPB) caliper is separated from the electric drive motor. Some manufacturers do not sell the components separately. Follow all service manual requirements prior to removal and during brake pad installation.

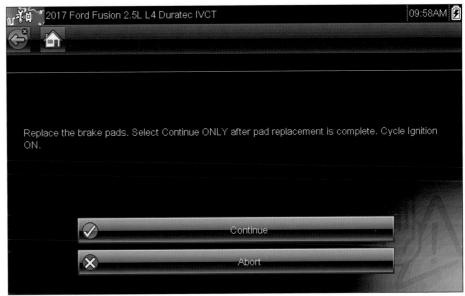

After the pads are installed, the scan tool reapplies the piston when prompted. Consult your vehicle's owner's manual or the service manual for further information. A special procedure known as a "work around" is sometimes possible, which does not require a scan tool.

This cutaway shows that this design uses metal gears to drive the corkscrew mechanism in the rear caliper that applies the parking brake. When rear brake replacement is required, the motor must retract the piston before the new pads can be installed.

HYDRAULIC BRAKE SYSTEMS

Early vehicles had mechanical brakes with metal rods pulling on levers to apply the brakes. Some had only rear brakes while others had brakes on all four wheels. When hydraulics were added to automotive brake systems, great improvements were made.

Operation

The advantages of using a hydraulic system to apply the brakes include the increase of force at the wheels by using different-size pistons, the ability to route around vehicle components, and the ability of flexible hoses to accommodate suspension and steering movement.

On the most basic system, when the brake pedal is pressed by your foot, a piston inside a cylinder bore in the master cylinder moves a column of brake fluid through metal lines and hoses to another piston, which converts the force back to mechanical to apply the brakes. If disc brakes are used, the output piston is larger to increase the clamping force on the brake pads. This is known as hydraulic advantage.

The amount of fluid movement is small because the system is com-

We are all used to seeing a master cylinder and vacuum booster hanging on the firewall of our daily driver, but early automobiles used mechanically actuated drum brake systems. When hydraulics were added, fluid movement took the place of mechanical movement. Because a fluid in a closed system cannot be compressed, fluid can do the same job as a mechanical rod; only better because of hydraulic advantage and routing solutions.

pletely full of fluid and if the pistons are the same diameter, whatever happens at the input end happens at the output end, even if the lines are 25 feet long. Although a common system may contain 2 to 4 pints of fluid, engineers have stated that only about 1 teaspoon of fluid moves in

the entire brake system when the pedal is depressed on a vehicle with four-wheel disc brakes and the pads may only move 0.003 inch to contact the rotors.

Fluid cannot be compressed and acts as a flexible solid inside a brake system. The French physicist and inventor Blaise Pascal stated back in the 1600s that hydraulic forces are equal within a system when pressure is applied to a confined fluid. Air, however, can compress and therefore must be kept out of the system for it to function properly. This is why brake bleeding must be done if the system was opened during service to remove all air from the system. Air in the fluid gives the brake pedal a spongy feeling as the air compresses and the fluid moves less, causing ineffective braking or even no braking.

Prior to 1967, most hydraulic systems used a single piston in the master cylinder to apply all four brakes.

In 1967, the US government mandated the use of dual-piston master cylinders to increase safety. One piston applies two wheels and another one applies the other two. If one system fails, the other provides some level of braking.

Most rear-wheel-drive vehicles have a front-to-rear split system, which means that one master cylinder piston applies the front brakes and the other applies the rears. Most front-wheel-drive vehicles use a diagonal split system, which means that one master cylinder piston applies the right front and left rear brakes and the other applies the left front and right rear brakes. The reason for this is that front-wheel-drive vehicles generally have less weight in the rear and need at least one front brake to stop if a partial brake system failure occurs. A feature built into the alignment geometry known as negative scrub radius helps keep the vehicle straight during braking on a diagonally split system when a partial hydraulic failure occurs.

Modern systems use the same

This 1952 Ford truck uses a single-piston master cylinder, which supplies fluid to all four wheels when the brake pedal is applied. A big disadvantage of this system is that a leak anywhere in the vehicle causes all brakes to fail. This is similar to the old Christmas light strands that were wired in series. When one bulb burned out, they all went out!

Beginning in 1967, government standards required the use of tandem master cylinders on vehicles. This design has a separate circuit for half of the vehicle and another for the other half. Older rear-wheel-drive models had one master cylinder piston for the front wheels and another for the rear wheels. Most front-wheel-drive vehicles use one circuit for one front wheel and one rear wheel and the other circuit for the other two wheels. This is known as being diagonally split.

design but incorporate ABS valves for proportioning and ABS/ADAS operation. In some cases, each brake can be controlled separately by a module using inputs from the wheels and from other sensors on the vehicle. Because of this, most manufacturers don't classify their vehicles as front-to-rear or diagonally split anymore. Any one of the four wheels can receive varying pressure depending on driving conditions and specific system design on many high-end and hybrid vehicles with electronic brake systems.

Caution: Many electronic and ABS systems use an HPA, which must be depressurized prior to hydraulic system service. This is accomplished by pumping the brake pedal as many as 40 times prior to opening the system. Check the service

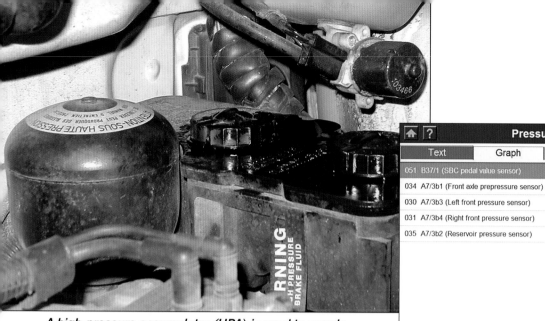

Pressures

Text	Graph	Graph merge	Analog

051 B37/1 (SBC pedal value sensor)	27.1	mm	
034 A7/3b1 (Front axle prepressure sensor)	28.5	bar	
030 A7/3b3 (Left front pressure sensor)	29.3	bar	
031 A7/3b4 (Right front pressure sensor)	28.5	bar	
035 A7/3b2 (Reservoir pressure sensor)	142.4	bar	

Esc Save Print Help To Top Pg Up Pg Dn

A high-pressure accumulator (HPA) is used to supply high-pressure brake fluid during ABS operation. Accumulators are also used with electronic brake systems. Most use a heavy rubber diaphragm with a charge of nitrogen gas inside. A pump motor in the modulator pressurizes the accumulator when the vehicle is started, and hydraulic valves open as necessary to supply the fluid to the wheels. Some must be depressurized before service.

Electronic brake systems develop extreme pressures that require special disabling procedures prior to service. Most use a scan tool to accomplish this. Do not make the mistake of thinking that if the key is off, you are safe! Specific methods must be followed for your safety. Some even require that the key be moved well away from the vehicle.

information on your vehicle for specific procedures prior to servicing the system.

Vehicles with electronic brakes may require a scan tool to disable the system because, even with the ignition off, some systems can perform a self-test at any time, sending HPA fluid into the system to check system integrity. This could apply the pistons and mash fingers! If the system is open for service, the high-pressure fluid could escape, causing severe injury. Refer to the service information for your vehicle prior to opening the system for service.

Electronic brake systems do not use a conventional master cylinder. Brake pressure is supplied by the electronic modulator for braking rather than the pressure being developed in the master cylinder. This allows precise pressure delivery to any wheel for varying conditions.

Master Cylinder

The master cylinder is the heart of most automotive hydraulic brake systems. It pushes hydraulic fluid to the wheels to apply the brakes like the human heart pushes blood to the body. It is mounted to the vehicle's bulkhead (firewall) and actuated by

A conventional master cylinder contains two pistons in a common bore that each supply pressure to two wheels when the brake pedal is applied. This particular unit has four ports, so it is used on a diagonally split system. A reservoir above the two pistons supplies fluid for the system. As the brake pads wear, the fluid in the reservoir drops because the caliper pistons must extend to take up the space.

a metal rod from the brake pedal or from the power booster. Some electronic brake systems do not use a traditional master cylinder. The pedal movement is monitored by hydraulic transducers that send electrical signals to a module, which supplies fluid pressure to the wheels.

The brake pedal is mounted with an offset pivot to gain a mechanical advantage and produce more leverage. A typical force of 100 pounds on the brake pedal is increased to about 500 pounds due to the offset.

The offset cannot be too great or the pedal must be moved excessively before the brakes apply, so the amount of assist is usually increased by using a vacuum booster between the brake pedal and the master cylinder. On some applications, the booster uses power steering pressure for assist. This type is known as hydroboost and is used on heavy-duty and diesel applications where adequate vacuum may not be available. A few models use an electric pump and high-pressure accumulator (HPA) for assist.

Components and Operation

Since 1967, master cylinders contain two pistons: primary and secondary. One sends fluid to two wheels and the other sends fluid to the other two wheels. Each piston presses against a cup seal when the brakes are applied to move the fluid along. These seals work similarly to an open umbrella inside of a piece of pipe. If you pull on the umbrella handle, the umbrella expands open and seals itself inside the pipe. Pushing on the handle causes the umbrella to close and move away from the pipe's

interior, allowing it to return to its original position.

Springs inside the master cylinder return both pistons to their original position when the brake pedal is released so that the vehicle is ready for the next stop.

A reservoir of fresh brake fluid is located above the master cylinder piston chambers and passages lead to both the primary and secondary pistons.

If the fluid level is low, a leak could be present in the system or the brake pads have worn enough that fluid has

The cup seals do not build pressure until they have each passed the vent ports in the bore of the master cylinder. At rest, the system is open between the wheels and the master cylinder reservoir, but when the brake pedal is pressed, the circuits seal and build pressure to the wheels.

Most vehicles use an offset brake pedal lever that pushes a rod into the master cylinder or power booster when the brakes are applied. There are adjustments for the amount of free play required. Refer to your vehicle's service information for specifics.

This illustration shows how the cup seals in a master cylinder operate. An open umbrella inside of a piece of pipe tries to open more when it is pulled through forcefully, making it seal better inside the pipe. A master cylinder cup seal works in the same way. High brake pedal force causes the cup to seal against the inside of the master cylinder bore. After the cup seal passes the vent port (top opening), it can then build pressure to the wheels.

The lid of the master cylinder reservoir must allow pressure to equalize as the brake fluid level drops without allowing air into the system. This is accomplished by a rubber diaphragm in the cap or a lid that can telescope into the reservoir. A small hole above the diaphragm allows air to enter through the cap or lid.

Be sure to push the rubber lid or cap seal back into its original position when the lid is removed for inspection or refilling of the fluid. Failure to do this causes fluid to spill over when the lid or cap is installed.

taken the place of the wear behind the caliper pistons. Some applications have a fluid level sensor in the master cylinder reservoir that monitors fluid level and illuminates the red brake warning lamp (RBWL) on the instrument panel when the fluid is low. This lamp can also be on if the parking brake is applied or the vehicle has a leak that caused a hydraulic imbalance in the system due to the action of the pressure differential switch. It could also be illuminated due to normal brake pad wear, but regardless of the cause, an RBWL should be addressed immediately because a safety issue may be present.

The lid or cap on the reservoir has a telescopic rubber seal under it. This seal allows air to be above it from a pinhole in the lid and fluid to move freely into the system below it without air being exposed to the fluid. When refilling the master cylinder, be sure to compress the telescopic seal into place so that it can extend again when the fluid is used

by the system. Do not overfill the reservoir.

If the fluid cannot expand due to the reservoir being overfilled when the system heats up, the brakes may drag or lock on as a result.

If the reservoir cap gasket is swollen, it is likely that someone mistak-

enly poured motor oil, transmission fluid, or some other petroleum-based fluid into the master cylinder.

To test the fluid, fill a cup or baby food jar with water and put about one teaspoon of fluid from the suspect master cylinder reservoir into the water and mix. Let it sit about one

If the rubber is distorted or swollen it is likely that some petroleum-based liquid has been accidently added to the brake system and all rubber parts in the system require replacement. This includes the master cylinder, ABS unit, hoses, calipers, and wheel cylinders. This is a fairly common mistake due to the various reservoirs being close together under the hood on some vehicles.

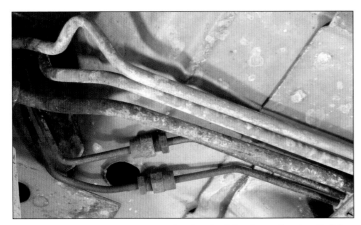

The metal lines need to be flushed with clean brake fluid prior to installing the new parts. If the lines are rusty, this is a great time to replace them. Do not use alcohol for flushing the lines because it is difficult to remove it all and it is flammable.

This master cylinder cutaway shows the two pistons and ports that supply fluid from the reservoir. These ports are known as the vent and replenishing ports. The vent port (with pointer) allows fluid to return from the wheels when the brakes are released. The replenishing port keeps the area behind the piston cups full of fluid so that no air can enter the system when the brakes are released.

To test for petroleum-based fluid in the brake fluid, put a sample in a jar with water and mix. Let it stand overnight. If there is a parting line and two different colors are evident in the jar, something other than brake fluid has been added to the system. Conventional brake fluid is miscible, which means that it mixes with water. Petroleum products are not, and neither is DOT 5 silicone fluid.

hour and then look for any film on the top of the water. Pure brake fluid mixes with the water and leaves no residue or film on the top of the sample (except for DOT 5 silicone fluid, which is purple).

Every rubber part in the hydraulic system must be replaced if petroleum-based fluid enters the system. This includes the master cylinder, calipers, wheel cylinders, hoses, ABS unit, and any other hydraulic valves. The lines must be flushed with clean brake fluid until all contamination has been removed. This is an expensive mistake.

In the master cylinder bore near the cup seals are ports leading from the master cylinder reservoir. There is one port on each side of both the primary and secondary cup seals. One is referred to as the vent port and the other is the replenishing port.

The vent port allows fluid to pass between the master cylinder reservoir and the system all the way to the wheels when the brakes are not applied. This is necessary because braking causes heat to increase at the wheels and the fluid expands.

Without the vent port allowing fluid escape during heat expansion, the brakes lock on. As soon at the pedal is applied, the cup seals move past the vent ports and push pressurized fluid to the wheels. In other words, the system can build pressure when the brakes are applied and can vent pressure to the reservoir when the brakes are not applied.

The replenishing port also has an important job. It allows fluid to occupy the area behind each cup seal. When the brakes are released, the return springs push the pistons back as quickly as possible to be ready for the next stop. This action causes the cup seals to collapse, somewhat like the umbrella inside of the pipe mentioned earlier. If air were present ahead of the cup seal, it would enter the hydraulic system

when the brakes were released and cause problems. The replenishing port keeps this area full of fluid; the only thing that goes around the partially collapsed cup seal when the brake is released is fluid. This area is not under pressure at any time on a common master cylinder (except fast-fill master cylinders).

Diagnosis

When a master cylinder fails, it is generally due to a damaged cup seal. This can occur over time as the cup seal moves back and forth over the vent port or it can fail due to improper bleeding methods.

When bleeding brakes, it is important not to push the brake pedal farther than it usually goes. A small buildup or ring of contamination can develop where the cup seals normally stop during braking over time. This is similar to an engine with a cylinder ridge from many years of operation. If the piston in an engine is forced past the ridge without removing it with a ridge reamer first, the piston or rings are damaged as the piston is driven out.

Likewise, in a master cylinder, if the cup seal is forced past the contamination line during brake bleeding, it can be damaged and develop a tear. A good way to prevent this is to put one foot under the brake pedal when bleeding so that it cannot go too far.

The most common symptom when a torn cup seal is present is the brake pedal slowly sinking to the floor at a stop light with light pedal pressure. The vehicle sometimes starts moving unless the pedal is released and reapplied with extra force. Many times, the brakes work fine during normal stopping with higher pedal effort because the cup seal is expanding more and sealing the damaged area. As soon as the pedal force is reduced, fluid begins to

leak around the damaged area of the cup seal (known as bypassing) and the pedal slowly creeps to the floor.

A similar symptom can appear due to a leak in the system, but the fluid level would be low and fluid would be found under the vehicle. The important distinction is that the fluid level remains intact if the master cylinder is bypassing.

It is normal to see turbulence in the fluid reservoir if the brake pedal is applied with the lid or caps removed. This is *not* an indication of master cylinder failure, and it is never wise to apply the brakes harshly with the lid off. Brake fluid can spray out and damage paint or cause a safety hazard.

A master cylinder can also develop an external leak where it bolts to the power booster. If fluid is present running down the booster or paint is blistered below the master cylinder on the power booster, fluid has likely entered the booster and both components should be replaced.

Service

In the past when a master cylinder failed, it was disassembled, the bore was honed, and a rebuild kit was installed containing new cup seals and O-rings. Today, most technicians install a new unit due to their reasonable cost and time savings. In the case of antique or specialty vehicles, rebuilding the existing master cylinder may make more sense due to parts availability and cost issues.

Prior to installation, you need to bench bleed the master cylinder to remove air from the new unit. The most effective method is to mount the new master cylinder in a vise by one of the attaching ears. Install fittings in the outlet ports with hoses leading to the reservoir. (A kit is sometimes supplied with the new master cylinder with fittings and clear tubing.) Fill the reservoir with the correct brake fluid and actuate the pistons with a wooden dowel or large Phillips screwdriver in 1-inch strokes until no air is seen in the hoses. You can also use your fingers

When bleeding a master cylinder, be careful not to depress the pedal too far. If the pistons go farther than they usually do when driving, the cup seals may be forced through internal contamination that could damage them. One trick is to put your other foot under the pedal when bleeding the brakes. A piece of a 2 x 4 can also be used for this purpose.

To replace the master cylinder, first crack loose the brake lines then snug them to avoid leakage. Loosen the two nuts (usually 15 mm) on the studs coming from the power booster. If you see any evidence of brake fluid under the master cylinder on the booster, the booster may also need replacement.

After the two nuts attaching the master cylinder to the booster and the lines are removed, the master cylinder can be slid forward away from the booster. Be careful not to allow any dripping fluid to come in contact with painted surfaces.

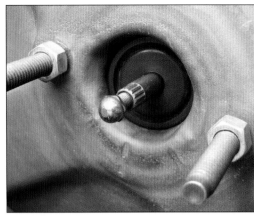

An adjustable pushrod is found sometimes between the master cylinder and the brake booster. This adjustment is critical because if it is too long, the brakes drag and lock up. This is due to the vent ports in the master cylinder being covered and not able to vent fluid back to the reservoir when the brakes are released. Refer to factory service information for adjustment methods when replacing a master cylinder.

to cover the ports when the pistons are released to keep air from sucking in if you don't have the hose kit, but this method is messy. This process ensures that the master cylinder is free of air.

Leave the hoses attached or cap off the ports. Put a rag under the unit and take it to the vehicle. Installing the unit is pretty easy, but be sure that the pushrod between the master cylinder and brake booster is properly seated and adjusted or brake lockup or failure can occur. Be sure that the lines are started before the master cylinder is completely secured to allow some movement to avoid stripping the line threads.

After installation on the vehicle, line bleed the unit before proceeding. This can be accomplished by having an assistant press lightly on the brake pedal while you loosen the lines with a shop towel under them. Be sure to retighten them prior to the pedal being released or air will re-enter the system. Do this at each line connec-

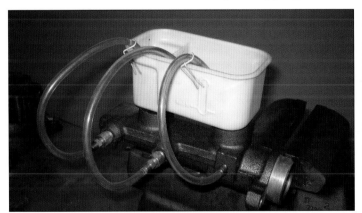

A new master cylinder is empty and must be bench bled prior to installation. Mount it in a vise by one of the mounting ears and attach clear plastic hoses and fittings into the master cylinder ports. Place the other end of the tubing in the reservoir and fill it with clean brake fluid. Using a wooden dowel or Phillips screwdriver, press in and out on the piston about 1 inch repeatedly until no air bubbles are seen in the plastic hoses.

After the master cylinder is installed on the vehicle, place a rag under the fittings and remove the plastic hoses and fittings. Attach the brake lines to the master cylinder and have an assistant press the pedal and crack open each bleeder to allow any trapped air to escape. This is known as line bleeding. It might be necessary to also bleed at the wheels if the lines have air in them.

tion until no air bubbles are present.

Wheel bleeding may be necessary if air entered the system.

Hydraulic Valves

Older brake systems used hydraulic valves to control flow or pressure within the system. These may include proportioning, metering, and pressure differential valves. In addition, pressure sensors may be used to alert the driver to problems within the system. On later models, an ABS modulator containing multiple valves may be used to replace the separate valves found on earlier designs. Electronic brake systems may contain even more sensors and valves within the electronic modulator.

Proportioning Valve

Older vehicles and many light trucks used mechanical proportioning valves in the hydraulic line between the master cylinder and the rear wheels to reduce rear brake pressure during panic stops. This was done to reduce rear wheel lockup, which could cause a loss of control especially when cornering on wet surfaces. This valve does not function during normal braking but can limit the pressure to the rear wheels in the range of 400–600 psi during a panic stop. The valve was generally mounted in a brass or aluminum housing with the metering valve and the pressure differential switch. Because three components were part of the assembly, it was referred to as a combination valve and usually mounted near the master cylinder on the frame rail.

Some pickups and SUVs on the road today still have this design. It is not serviceable and must be replaced as a unit if any of the components fail.

A combination valve (arrow) was used on older vehicles, which housed a proportioning valve, metering valve, and pressure differential switch. These valves were between the master cylinder and the wheels. The combination valve provided multiple functions, including alerting the driver of a leak that caused a hydraulic imbalance.

If the proportioning valve sticks closed, nosedive could occur and the vehicle could be more difficult to stop because the rear brakes do not function properly. The vehicle may also wear out front brakes abnormally fast. Rear brakes that are not functioning properly due to a proportioning valve failure usually have rust on the friction surface of the drum or rotor.

If the proportioning valve sticks open, the brakes function normally except during panic stops when rear brakes could lock up.

Some vehicles use a height-sensing proportioning valve. Mechanical linkage to the rear suspension opens hydraulic passages more when a load is applied to the rear of the vehicle for more rear braking. If the springs sag on the vehicle, it could develop rear brake lockup over time. Also, when bleeding it might be necessary to

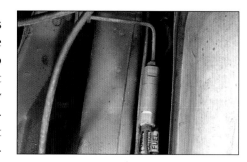

A proportioning valve is used on some applications between the master cylinder and the line(s) leading to the rear wheels. Its purpose is to reduce brake pressure to the rear wheels during panic stops and increase safety, especially when braking heavily on turns.

have the vehicle weight on the tires rather than in the air. On some applications, when the suspension is free hanging, the height-sensing proportioning valve completely closes off fluid to the rear wheels, preventing any attempt to bleed the rear brakes.

Some vehicles use a height-sensing proportioning valve. This type has a rod attached to a moveable arm, which regulates rear brake pressure based on chassis height. A heavy load causes the valve to open more, which supplies more pressure to the rear wheels. If the rear springs are sagged, the vehicle could have rear wheel lockup when unloaded. Unloaded suspension can cause issues during bleeding where a height-sensing valve is used.

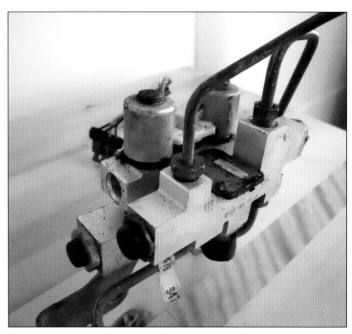

A metering valve between the master cylinder and the front wheels is commonly used on older vehicles with disc and drum brakes. Because disc brakes apply faster than drum brakes, the metering valve provides a slight delay in the pressure to the front wheels to eliminate nosedive.

Modern vehicles use more complex methods to reduce rear wheel lockup. The ABS system is often used to control proportioning by monitoring individual wheel speeds, vehicle speed, steering angle, and yaw rate. Some systems even control side-to-side bias electronically. Because of these advancements, the mechanical proportioning valve is not found on later vehicles, which reduces overall vehicle weight and makes the vehicle safer and more reliable.

Metering Valve

The metering valve is placed in the hydraulic line between the master cylinder and the front disc brakes when rear drum brakes are used. The purpose of this valve is to momentarily delay the front brakes to allow time for the rear brakes to apply. Due to design, the front disc brakes can apply quicker than the

rears because the pads are very close to the rotor surface. Drum brakes take a little more time to apply because the shoes are retracted by the return springs, leaving a larger gap between the shoes and the drums than the gap between the pads and rotor.

Without the metering valve, the vehicle tends to nosedive during braking due to the front brakes applying before the rears. If the valve is stuck closed, rear brake lockup is the symptom. If the valve is stuck open, nosedive occurs. In either case, the unit is not serviceable and must be replaced.

Pressure Differential Switch

The pressure differential switch can be part of the combination valve or it can be mounted in the master cylinder. It is a sliding piston that is balanced between the primary and secondary master cylinder circuits.

If a hydraulic imbalance occurs due to a leak in one of the circuits, the piston moves toward the side with the lowest pressure (leak side). The piston has a recess that is in contact with a push-button switch. This switch grounds the circuit, turning on the RBWL on the instrument panel if the piston moves to either side. This warns the driver of a partial brake failure.

On some applications, the piston seals off the leaking circuit to reduce fluid loss and improves pedal height when a partial brake failure occurs. Component parts to repair the pressure differential switch are usually not available; replacement is required if it fails. If it is part of a master cylinder or combination valve, the entire unit is usually replaced.

After a hydraulic imbalance occurs that illuminates the RBWL, the piston must be re-centered on most applications after the repairs are made. This can sometimes be accomplished by bleeding one channel and then the other to force the piston to re-center, but if it sticks, the unit must be replaced or the RBWL remains illuminated.

Most differential switches ground the circuit when the switch is on. Diagnosis is simple. Turn on the ignition switch. If the red lamp remains on, unplug the connector at the pressure differential switch. If the lamp goes out, the piston is not centered.

If the lamp stays on after the wire is unplugged, check the fluid level and see if the parking brake is on. If the lamp does not illuminate, ground the wire to see if it comes on with the key on. If it does not, a blown bulb, bad fuse, or circuit issue in the dash could be the issue.

Remember that the parking brake can also turn on the lamp if the parking brake is applied.

Some applications use a float switch in the fluid reservoir. When the fluid drops due to worn pads or a leak, the RBWL illuminates. On older GM trucks and vans with Kelsey-Hayes Rear Wheel Antilock (RWAL) ABS systems, the RBWL can be illuminated very dimly when an ABS fault exists. This bulb was also used to flash out codes.

Antilock Brake System

On most late-model vehicles, ABS has taken over the duties of brake bias to the front and rear during operation; mechanical proportioning, metering, and a pressure differential switch are not as common. See chapter 9 for more details.

Brake Lines

Brake lines are made of steel alloy and route the fluid from the master cylinder to the wheels. Some lines are coiled under the master cylinder to allow some movement because the master cylinder is attached to the body and the other components are attached to the frame with rubber bushings between them.

Copper should not be used as a brake line because it does not have the burst-pressure capacity of steel. Most replacement line is steel, but replacement line is available that is easier to work with and lasts longer. It is referred to as copper nickel, but it is approved for brake systems. Stainless steel line is also available for even more protection against rust, but it is not very flexible and harder to work with. Both copper nickel and stainless steel are more expensive than common steel line.

A typical brake system may have more than 1,200 psi in the lines to the front wheels during a panic stop, so lines should never be repaired with hose or compression fittings designed for low-pressure use. A common compression fitting from a hardware store is not designed to withstand the pressures inside of a brake system.

The most common reason for brake line failure is rust from road salt and moisture. This is especially true

A pressure differential switch is used on some models to alert the driver to a hydraulic imbalance in the system. This switch uses a piston in a bore with fluid pressure from one circuit on one side and pressure from the other circuit on the other side. If a difference exists, the piston moves and grounds a circuit to illuminate the RBWL.

Steel brake lines are used to route the hydraulic pressure to the wheels. They are located under the vehicle and are subject to adverse conditions such as water, salt, dust, and vibration. A thorough inspection should be made to ensure that the lines are in good condition.

on domestic pickup trucks and vans. In areas of snow and salt, moisture can attack the brake lines under the vehicle and this corrosion eventually leads to leaks. A common place for rust to develop is above the vehicle fuel tank and under clamps where dirt collects and water does not run off or evaporate easily. Another reason for line damage is abrasion due to improper routing or missing brackets, so if replacement is necessary, try your best to duplicate the factory routing and brackets.

The best repair includes total replacement of the affected line. If some lines are still intact you can install replacement sections to the next union or flare the existing line if it is intact. Use a union—not a compression fitting. Line is available in various lengths and with different flares on the ends. It is acceptable to use a union to attach two sections together, but it is not acceptable to use a common compression fitting due to the high pressure in the system.

Metric and standard line sections are available in various diameters and lengths. You can also purchase 25-foot rolls of brake line. If you make your own lines you will likely

Sections of brake line can be purchased in various lengths. Try to duplicate the factory routing and brackets to avoid interference- and vibration-related damage down the road. Several diameters are available; 3/16 and 1/4 inch are the most common. Some applications use metric lines, which are close in size to domestic.

When brake lines are found to be badly rusted or damaged, replacement is required. Do not use compression fittings or copper tubing because they cannot handle high pressures. Sections can be replaced, but factory-type flares and unions must be used. It might be necessary to replace the entire system in cases of extreme rust.

Pay special attention to the brake lines near brackets (arrow). Water can collect in these areas and cause rust to develop inside the bracket, causing a leak or restriction. If you are replacing the lines, be sure to route them as close to the factory path as possible.

Inspect the Brake System

I recently started on a trip with a car hauler trailer behind a full-size pickup truck. Coming up to a stop sign about 3 miles from home, the brake pedal went to the floor. Barely enough braking was available to bring the vehicle to a stop. Knowing that this type and brand of vehicle is notorious for rusted brake lines, I looked under the vehicle and saw brake fluid dripping from the metal line under the vehicle between the ABS modulator and the left front wheel.

I nursed the vehicle back home in low gear using the parking brake and managed to unhook the trailer and get a look underneath. Sure enough, the brake lines were rusted and leaking. Every line on the truck had been replaced about eight years prior, but the harsh winter conditions took their toll once again.

The lesson here is to periodically inspect the brake system before you get into a jam. ∎

reuse the old line nuts and make your own flares. If you need to reuse the old fittings, clean them up before cutting the line to remove them. This eliminates getting your fingers into the wire wheel used during cleaning. Fitting assortments are also available and separate fittings are available from parts stores.

Complete kits are available for vehicles that commonly rust, which may be less expensive than making the line yourself. Some are made of upgraded material for better resistance to rust.

If you must reuse the line nuts from the old lines and they are rusty, polish them up with a wire wheel on a bench grinder prior to cutting them off the lines. This allows them to spin when contacting the wire wheel without the wire wheel contacting the tips of your fingers.

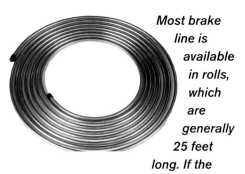

Most brake line is available in rolls, which are generally 25 feet long. If the vehicle has ABS and you are replacing the entire system, you can plan on using at least two rolls. Fabricating brake lines is a time-consuming job. Pre-bent, flared kits are available for many applications and can save time.

The Rule of Thirds

My current supervisor at our college has stated that a good flare is produced by one-third ability, one-third tool quality, and one-third luck. A wise man once said, "I have noticed that the harder I work, the luckier I get," so practice is what is necessary for producing a good flare. ∎

Line Flaring

Flared lines are used in brake systems. The two most common flares are double flare and ISO flare (also called bubble flare). With a good flaring kit, you can make the flares yourself. Tubing cutters and line-bending tools are also available. If the bend is not too tight, you can sometimes bend the line by hand. Be careful not to kink the line. A hydraulic hand-held flaring tool is also available in the aftermarket, but it is expensive.

Brake Hoses

Brake hoses attach between the metal brake lines and the suspension system to allow for movement during

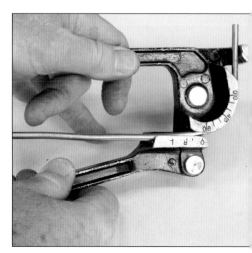

When bending tubing, a special bending tool should be used to avoid kinking the line. The tool can accomplish any angle in any direction. It takes a little getting used to, so use some of the old line to practice on.

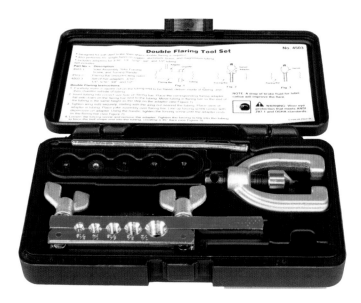

Flaring the tubing ends with a manual flaring tool is a cost-effective approach if you're planning to just make a few lines. It is, however, a more time-consuming and difficult method, especially if you're working under the vehicle. A drop of brake fluid on the tip of the line can help lubricate it during flaring.

To cut the tubing, a special tubing cutter must be used. A hacksaw should never be used to cut brake tubing. The cutter uses a sharp wheel that gradually cuts its way through the tubing as the tool is spun around the tubing and the cutter drive screw is tightened a little at a time.

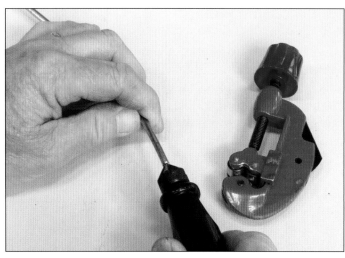

After the tubing is cut, it should be chamfered both internally and externally prior to flaring it. A double-ended reamer is available that can do the entire job. Clean the area before you start to flare the line.

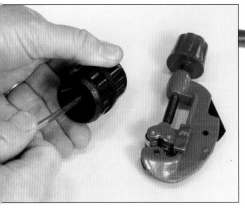

This tool is used to chamfer the outside of the tubing before using the flaring tool. This allows the flaring tool to seat better on the line and produce a better flare.

This is how a flare should look after using the flaring tool. It must look just like the OEM tubing or it might leak.

Two types of flares are used on modern vehicles. The most common on domestic vehicles is the double flare. Many imports use an ISO flare, but you may find either or both on nearly any vehicle. Special tools are available to make the flares. This tool uses a pump-up handle to apply hydraulic force. It works well and is portable for use under the vehicle but has a fairly high cost.

chassis deflection and when steering. They are high-pressure hoses and must be handled with care. To avoid damage to the hose, do not clamp it or allow the caliper to hang from it during service.

The hose has several layers of rubber and fabric material with a hard plastic inner liner that can crack if it is severely kinked or clamped off. Clamping off the hose during service or diagnosis is not recommended, even with special tools, because the clamping forces can cause a fracture and internal damage to the nylon sleeve that can act as a "one-way flapper valve," either keeping the brakes on or keeping them from working on that wheel. It can also cause a bubble to develop as the high pressure seeps into the weaker hose wall.

Also be careful not to twist the hose as the caliper is installed. A twist can cause the hose to pull apart when turning and lose hydraulic pressure.

Banjo Fitting

A banjo fitting is used on most vehicles where the brake hose attaches to the calipers. It uses a hollow bolt and a copper washer on each side of the fitting to seal the connection. The name comes from the fact that the end of the hose has a metal fitting that resembles a tiny banjo.

The line must be in the proper position before tightening the bolt, so pay attention to its position before removal. The torque on this bolt is important. If it is too loose, it will certainly leak and it could break if too tight due to being hollow, so use a torque wrench when installing it.

The copper washers are supposed to be replaced if the connection is removed. The old ones tend to stick to the bolt and fitting. If the banjo fitting is removed, brake fluid drips out and eventually empties the master cylinder. This is why some technicians clamp off the hose, which can damage it. A much better idea is to use a tire valve stem to seal the hose where the banjo bolt was.

The end that attaches the hose to the brake caliper usually has a connection known as a banjo fitting. It uses a hollow bolt and two copper washers for sealing the high pressure. It must be installed in the proper position so that it does not kink when the vehicle is steered, so pay close attention to the old one if you remove it.

Because the bolt that attaches the banjo fitting to the brake caliper is hollow and compresses two copper washers, it is important to torque it to manufacturer's specifications. If it is overtightened, it could break. If too loose, it leaks brake fluid. Torque specifications are found in the service information for your vehicle.

Brake hoses are used to allow flexibility for suspension movement and steering. These hoses contain multiple layers for the strength needed to withstand high brake pressures sometimes in excess of 1,200 pounds. Be sure to thoroughly inspect all hoses for cracks or damage. Any crack that exposes inner fabric means that the hose should be replaced.

Wheel Cylinders

Wheel cylinders are positioned between the two brake shoes to push them into the inside of the spinning drum to stop the vehicle. They contain two pistons and cup seals along with an internal spring and dust seals.

Pressurized brake fluid inside the wheel cylinder pushes the pistons into the shoes. Some applications use short pushrods between the pistons and shoes. The backside of the wheel cylinder has the line connection and a bleeder screw above it to remove air trapped inside during bleeding.

Wheel cylinders can develop leaks over time that can cause the shoes to be contaminated with fluid. If a wheel cylinder is dripping, it needs to be rebuilt or replaced. Most shops replace rather than rebuild today. This is partially due to labor cost and time savings, but honing the inside can remove special coatings that are present, especially on aluminum wheel cylinders.

Replacement is relatively simple after the shoes are removed or pried away. Two bolts or a ring usually hold the wheel cylinder to the backing plate and the line threads into the unit just below the bleeder screw. Be careful not to cross-thread the line during installation. It is easier to attach the line finger tight prior to mounting the unit to the backing plate and then install the retaining bolts. When installing a wheel cylinder, be sure to position it so that the brake bleeder is at the top. This allows the air to escape during bleeding after the job. Although rare, some vehicles have wheel cylinders that can be installed upside down or on the wrong side of the vehicle.

Brake Calipers

Brake calipers contain pistons that extend against the pads causing clamping of the rotor to stop the vehicle when the brakes are applied. A brake pad on each side of the rotor is held in position within the caliper. Brake calipers serve the same purpose in disc brakes as the wheel cylinder serves in drum brakes. Brake caliper pistons must be returned into

their bores prior to the installation of new brake pads. Rear disc calipers sometimes have a drive screw for the parking brakes, which means that the piston must be rotated as it is returned into the bore.

Brake Fluid

The most common brake fluid in use today is DOT 3. Some older vehicles with four-wheel-drum

Inside of a wheel cylinder you find two small pistons with cup seals and a spring between them. Two dust boots keep contamination away from the pistons and seals. If a wheel cylinder is leaking, most professionals replace it rather than rebuilding it due to low cost and parts availability.

DOT 3 in Old European Vehicles Can Cause Trouble

Some old European vehicles used a vegetable-based fluid that cannot be mixed with any other fluid. Girling was a common manufacturer of this fluid. If common DOT 3 fluid is put into this system, all rubber components swell, and the brakes eventually lock on when applied. I experienced this at a young age when helping a friend with the brakes and clutch on his father's 1963 Triumph TR-3. ■

Brake calipers use hydraulic pressure from the master cylinder to squeeze two brake pads around the rotor when the brakes are applied. Calipers are bolted to the steering knuckle or a bracket attached to the steering knuckle. They contain one or more pistons that can be made of steel, aluminum, or phenolic material.

Be sure to check the lid of the master cylinder reservoir or service information to determine which brake fluid to use in your vehicle. DOT 3 is the most common but many vehicles, especially European vehicles, use DOT 4, which has a higher boiling point. There are fluids with even higher boiling points, such as DOT 5.1 for racing. DOT 5 has a high boiling point but is silicone based and should not be mixed with other fluids or be used in any vehicle with ABS.

Technically speaking, you could use a fluid with a higher boiling point than the fluid listed for your vehicle, but it is wise to stick with the fluid specified by the manufacturer to make sure it is compatible with all of the internal components. Some manufacturers do not allow a higher DOT fluid.

Most shops use brake-fluid test strips to determine fluid condition. These strips can check for copper present in the fluid, which leaches from the steel as the fluid ages. This gives a good indication of fluid age and additive depletion. The strip is dipped in the master cylinder reservoir and then left on a shop towel for a short period of time. The color indicates whether or not fluid replacement is recommended.

Another way to test brake fluid is to use a tool that boils a sample of the fluid to detect its boiling point. It is often referred to as moisture testing. The tester attaches to the vehicle battery and is placed in the master cylinder reservoir. This method has largely been replaced with test strips. Some now regard this test as being inadequate.

Some shops use a brake fluid flushing machine to completely flush the system. It is attached to a sealed cap on the master cylinder reservoir and pressurizes the entire system. A hose is connected to the bleeder and returns the dirty fluid to a container on the machine. The brakes may also be bled manually until clean fluid emits from each bleeder.

systems used DOT 2, which is no longer available. Some high-heat applications, such as police, ambulance, and German cars, use DOT 4. All of these amber colored fluids are glycol based and can damage painted surfaces quickly.

They are also miscible, which means that they mix with water. This may seem like a bad thing, but you don't want water separating in the lowest points of the system, especially when the weather is below freezing! DOT 3 and DOT 4 have different boiling points and therefore should not be interchanged. You can never use a fluid with a lower temperature rating than used by the vehicle manufacturer. Look at the master cylinder reservoir cap to determine the proper fluid to use.

Keep the lid of the master cylinder and your bottle of brake fluid closed as much as possible because brake fluid absorbs moisture from the atmosphere quickly. DOT 5 fluid is silicone based and often purple in color. It doesn't damage paint like the others and has a high boiling point. It is often used in high-performance vehicles, but it has some disadvantages. It does not mix with water and can foam when used in ABS-equipped vehicles due to the rapid valve movement in the ABS modulator. Therefore it cannot be used in a vehicle that has ABS.

A relatively new fluid has been developed called DOT 5.1. It has the same boiling point as DOT 5 without the disadvantages, although it does damage paint.

Fluid Flushing

Some vehicle manufacturers suggest the brake fluid should be flushed and refilled at specific intervals related to mileage or time, but most manufacturers suggest fluid replacement only when the system is opened for service. Check your owner's manual or the service information for your vehicle to determine the manufacturer's recommendations. Most experts, such as Motorist Assurance

Program (MAP), suggest periodic flushing since brake fluid can absorb moisture and degrade over time and the additives can become depleted. This can cause brake fade when the system becomes hot and the pedal could sink until the fluid cools.

Hydraulic parts fail due to time, not mileage, so a vehicle that sits for extended periods of time could end up with leaks, stuck valves, and internal corrosion or contamination. It is not good to let a vehicle sit.

If a system is contaminated, only brake fluid should be used to flush the system. Denatured alcohol can be used to clean disassembled parts but should never be used to flush a brake system because some will likely remain in the system, creating a potential for brake failure.

Test strips and other devices can be used for testing brake fluid to determine whether or not it needs to be flushed. Some test for copper content and others test for moisture content. Moisture content testing, which typically boil a fluid sample to determine the level of water intrusion, has largely been replaced with copper content testing because it has been found to be more accurate at determining fluid quality.

The Society of Automotive Engineers (SAE) endorses the copper content test and most professionals use test strips for that purpose. The

strips change color after being dipped in the fluid after a minute or so if the fluid has high copper content indicating the need to flush.

Copper is one of the components in steel brake lines, and the copper leaches into the fluid over time. Measuring its content is a good way to determine the age of the fluid, which is an indicator of additive depletion levels. The SAE suggests no more than 200 ppm (parts per million) of copper in a modern hydraulic brake system.

Some shops use brake fluid flush machines that install the fluid under low pressure into the master cylinder while the bleeder is opened at each wheel to return the dirty fluid to a second tank on the machine. Other shops use gravity and foot bleeding to accomplish this task. Vacuum bleeders are also available, which attach to the bleeders and pull fresh fluid from the master cylinder into the system and out the bleeder.

Bleeding the System

Air in the brake system causes a spongy pedal and affects braking ability. If there is enough air, you won't have any brakes at all. One thing for sure, you cannot have *any* air in the hydraulic system anywhere if you are planning on them working as they were designed to, so bleeding is required after service.

Also during a brake job, you likely have the hydraulic system open for service and want to have new fluid in the new components. A good first step is to use a turkey baster to remove the old fluid from the master cylinder reservoir and replace it with new fluid. Be careful not to allow any fluid onto painted surfaces. Brake fluid is very damaging to paint.

A good "first step" before a brake job is to remove all of the old fluid from the master cylinder reservoir with a turkey baster or vacuum bleeder. Replace it with new fluid prior to beginning work at the wheels so that nothing but fresh, clean fluid flows through the system and ABS unit when you open up the hydraulic system downstream.

Any of several methods can be used to bleed air out of a vehicle brake system.

Foot Bleeding

Foot bleeding is probably the most common method used in the home garage. It is quick and effective and does not require a lot of special equipment, just an assistant, the right fluid, drip pans, and some wrenches to open and close the bleeders. Make sure all bleeders are closed and the master cylinder reservoir is full of fluid before you start.

Have your assistant press down on the brake pedal about halfway by saying "down" and then open the right rear bleeder with a pan below. Close the bleeder and tell your assistant to release the pedal by saying "up." Wait a few seconds and repeat the process until clean fluid is coming from the bleeder with no air bubbles. A solid, clean stream of fluid

Be sure to place a pan under the wheel you are bleeding to catch the old brake fluid and avoid a mess on the floor. Continue bleeding until fresh fluid comes from the bleeder and no air bubbles are present. Good communication with your assistant is critical here so that he or she does not release the pedal with the bleeder open. Be sure to clean the components afterward so that brake fluid does not drip on the floor or end up on painted surfaces.

indicates you can move on to the next wheel.

Generally you begin with the wheel farthest from the master cylinder (right rear, or RR) and work your way to the closest. This means that on front to rear split systems (most rear-wheel-drive vehicles), the pattern is RR, LR, RF, LF. On diagonally split systems (most front-wheel-drive vehicles), the pat-

tern is RR, LF, LR, RF. The sequence may vary. Check service information. Be sure to check the master cylinder reservoir fluid level from time to time so that it doesn't go dry and top it off to the maximum line when finishing.

Gravity Bleeding

Gravity bleeding works exclusively with gravity. The master

Foot bleeding is the most common way to bleed a brake system and is very effective but requires two people. An assistant presses down on the pedal and you open and close the bleeders to allow the air to escape. Common mistakes include pressing the pedal too far and causing master cylinder damage or releasing the pedal while the bleeder is open, allowing air to be sucked back into the system.

Gravity bleeding is a method that allows gravity to pull fluid from the system to each bleeder and can be performed by one person. Pans are placed at all four corners of the vehicle and all bleeders are opened after filling the master cylinder reservoir. Some vehicles do not gravity bleed due to system design. It is always wise to foot bleed afterward to ensure that a good pedal exists and no air is present.

cylinder is filled and the bleeders are opened with pans under them to allow gravity to pull the fresh fluid from the master cylinder and throughout the system. When clean fluid emerges from the bleeders, the system is full of new fluid.

It is wise to foot bleed the system afterward to ensure that all air is removed and the pedal height and feel is correct. Be sure to check the master cylinder reservoir fluid level from time to time so that it doesn't go dry and top it off to the maximum line when finished.

Pressure Bleeding

Pressure bleeding requires a special tank that attaches to the reservoir of the master cylinder and feeds new brake fluid under pressure into the reservoir. It contains a diaphragm charged with low-pressure shop air. Each bleeder can be opened with a pan underneath and fluid flows until it is clear. This method requires only one person but the pressure bleeder is costly and adapters are not always available to allow attachment to your master cylinder reservoir cap or lid. Leaks are common around the reservoir seals with these systems, which can cause fluid to spray onto painted surfaces.

Vacuum Bleeding

Most vacuum bleeders attach to shop air and create a venturi effect to pull fluid through the system and out of each bleeder. Begin by filling the master cylinder reservoir with new fluid. Attach the rubber coupler from the vacuum bleeder hose to a bleeder and then open it about one turn. Turn on the vacuum bleeder and watch for a column of fluid to flow into the vacuum bleeder reservoir bottle.

It is not uncommon to see some bubbles because air can be sucked in around the bleeder threads. To eliminate this, you can apply a small amount of silicone brake grease around the threads of the bleeder.

Be sure to check the master cylinder reservoir fluid level from time to time so that it doesn't go dry and top it off to the maximum line when finished.

The pressure bleeding method attaches a sealed cap with a hose to the master cylinder reservoir. The unit has a bladder that uses air pressure to force brake fluid through the hose and into the system. Each bleeder is opened and fluid is allowed to flow until it is clean and free of air bubbles. This method requires only one person. A variety of adapters are required for attachment to all of the various master cylinder reservoirs.

Vacuum bleeding has become more popular in many shops. It uses shop air to create a vacuum on a pump that contains a reservoir for the old fluid. A clear plastic hose attaches to the open bleeder and sucks the fluid through the system from the master cylinder until clean fluid is seen in the hose. One drawback is that air bubbles are in the hose at all times due to air being sucked in around the open bleeder threads. This can make it difficult to determine when all the air has been removed from the system. Silicone grease on the threads may help.

Surge Bleeding

Surge bleeding allows you to bleed the brakes alone using a jar or bottle and a hose. Start by gravity bleeding all wheels until clean fluid drips at all four corners. Fill the jar with new brake fluid and be sure the hose is totally immersed in the fluid through the lid. Attach the other end of the hose to the open bleeder and hang the jar or bottle by its hook near the wheel.

For surge bleeding, a hose is attached to the bleeder leading to a sealed jar. The pedal is lightly pumped up and down until clean fluid with no bubbles is seen in the jar of new brake fluid. It is important to make sure the hose in the jar is covered by clean brake fluid at all times. You may also find it helpful to apply some silicone brake grease around the threads of the open bleeder so that air is not sucked back in during the process.

Slowly depress the brake pedal about halfway and then slowly release it. Continue this process for several strokes to ensure that all air has been expelled into the jar or bottle. Close the bleeder and move on to the next closest hydraulic channel until you have bled all wheels.

Be sure to check the master cylinder reservoir fluid level from time to time so that it doesn't go dry and top it off to the maximum line when finished.

Automated Bleeding

Some scan tools can use the ABS system to pump fluid through the system to aid in removing air, especially from the ABS unit itself. If a line rusts through and all the fluid leaks out of the system, air can enter the ABS, which can be difficult to remove.

Scan tool methods known as "automated bleed" or "hydraulic function test" run the pump motor with the brake pedal depressed and actuate the hydraulic valves one at a time to rid the unit of air. The pedal generally moves up and down four or five times as the pump runs. The scan tool then instructs you to bleed the system at the wheels and test drive the vehicle.

If a scan tool is not available, and you can get a safe pedal, you might be able to perform a couple of ABS stops in a nearby parking lot by driving through water or gravel and applying the brakes harshly. This action causes an ABS stop as long as the system is functioning and the ABS light is off. It causes the pump and valves to operate similarly to the scan tool process and can aid in removing air from the ABS unit.

Be sure that the vehicle is safe to drive before attempting this! If in doubt, obtain a scan tool or have the vehicle towed to a shop that has one.

On late-model vehicles with ABS or electronic systems or if a vehicle had a severe leak that emptied the system, it might be necessary to use a scan tool during bleeding. It is sometimes difficult to fill empty lines due to an issue similar to vapor lock in a fuel system. Pressure may be the only way to push the air out.

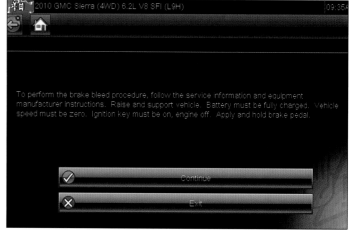

The scan tool often has an "automated bleed" mode that can command the electric pump to engage and the solenoids to open in a sequence that removes all air from the ABS or electronic brake unit. This method often requires pedal application while following scan tool commands.

BRAKE ASSIST SYSTEMS

Before power brakes became common in the early 1970s, vehicles had manual brakes and most had four-wheel drum systems. Early models used metal rods instead of hydraulics to apply the brakes. One way to increase brake force was to increase the length of the brake arm going to the pedal for more leverage, but this required more pedal movement before the brakes applied.

Adding hydraulics allowed the use of hydraulic advantage, which uses a smaller diameter input piston pressing on a larger diameter output piston. A modern example is a master cylinder piston with a 1-inch diameter pressing on a disc brake caliper piston of 3 inches in diameter and greatly increasing the force on the pads to stop the wheel. The output piston moves one-third the distance with three times the force.

This was a major improvement over mechanical brake operation, but it still required fairly strong effort on the brake pedal. When power-assisted brakes were

When a master cylinder has a smaller bore than the brake caliper, hydraulic advantage causes more force in the caliper than the force applied by the driver. If the caliper piston is three times larger than the master cylinder piston, it moves one-third the distance but has three times the output force on the pads.

One of these levers on this 1952 Ford truck leads from the brake pedal to the master cylinder. This vehicle has no power brakes, so the lever is highly offset to provide a mechanical advantage and increase brake force to the master cylinder. The other lever is the clutch pedal lever.

You can see that the piston in the caliper is much larger than the diameter of the master cylinder in the previous photo. This is referred to as hydraulic advantage and greatly increases the force from the driver's foot to the brake pads.

Most vehicles use a vacuum power booster between the brake pedal and master cylinder. It uses engine vacuum against a large rubber diaphragm to increase the force into the master cylinder. When a vehicle is decelerating, vacuum is at its highest, which is used with atmospheric pressure on the other side of the diaphragm to provide brake assist.

This is a typical power booster, master cylinder, and pushrod. These components mount on the vehicle's firewall (bulkhead) and connect to the brake pedal linkage. Each combination of booster and master cylinder is engineered for the specific vehicle.

introduced, nearly anyone had the strength to stop a large vehicle.

Power brakes are found on virtually all newer vehicles and most use a vacuum or hydraulic assist unit to increase the driver's pedal force going into the master cylinder. The booster is generally mounted on the bulkhead (firewall) and the master cylinder bolts to it with a short pushrod between them.

The input end of the booster attaches to the brake pedal. When the driver applies the brakes, the booster increases the force going into the master cylinder to reduce the amount of pedal effort required. The booster uses engine vacuum to increase the assist, but some applications use pressurized fluid from the power steering pump. Some later models use a pump motor and hydraulic accumulator to store the pressurized fluid needed to apply the brakes and apply electronically from a module that monitors the brake pedal position and force with sensors. These are generically referred to as electronic brake systems (covered later in this chapter) and are found on high-end vehicles and many hybrids.

Vacuum

The most common type of brake assist is the vacuum-balanced booster design. If you are familiar with choke pull-offs on carburetor-equipped vehicles, you have a pretty good idea of how a vacuum power booster works. The difference is that vacuum is present on both sides of the diaphragm until the brake pedal is applied.

A power booster can be compared to a vacuum actuator on an old carburetor (arrow).

When vacuum is applied to the diaphragm inside the actuator, an attached rod (arrow) actuates the component. A vacuum booster works in a similar way but uses atmospheric pressure on the other side of the diaphragm to increase the assist even more.

A vacuum booster is a large housing containing a rubber diaphragm and valving to increase the force from the brake pedal to the master cylinder. It uses engine vacuum to provide the force, which is a byproduct of engine operation. Vacuum boost systems do not affect fuel economy.

This cutaway shows the internal components of a vacuum balanced power booster. When the brakes are not applied, engine vacuum is present on both sides of the diaphragm (arrow). When the pedal is depressed, atmospheric pressure takes the place of the vacuum on the driver's side of the diaphragm and force increases on the rod leading to the master cylinder.

Vacuum is applied to a large rubber diaphragm inside the booster to greatly increase the brake force from the driver to the master cylinder. The diameter of the diaphragm is large enough to create great force on the master cylinder. If extra force is needed and space is at a minimum, two diaphragms can be used in the same housing. The setup is known as a tandem design.

How It Works

The vacuum-balanced booster is the most common design. Atmospheric pressure is almost 15 pounds per square inch at sea level and engine vacuum at idle is usually 20 inches or so. It is even higher when the vehicle is decelerating. A hose from the intake manifold leads to a one-way check valve on the booster housing. This "failsafe" valve retains vacuum in the booster in case the engine stalls so that at least two assisted stops are available. Engine vacuum is applied to each side of the diaphragm when your foot is off the brake pedal.

A sliding spool valve in the middle of the diaphragm controls the assist function. When the brakes are applied, the sliding spool valve closes off the flow between the two sides of the diaphragm and opens a filtered passage for atmospheric air from under the instrument cluster to enter the rear side of the diaphragm. The other side of the diaphragm closest to the master cylinder still has manifold vacuum, so it greatly increases the force on the rod leading to the master cylinder.

A vacuum check valve in the hose leading from the intake manifold to the power booster ensures that at least two assisted stops are available if the engine dies. This valve allows flow in one direction but not the other. If you remove it from the power booster and start the engine, you should feel engine vacuum when putting your finger over the hole.

A foam filter (arrow) is used on the atmospheric passage of the vacuum booster to protect the internal components. Heavy smoking by the driver can clog this filter and reduce brake assist over time.

The engine must be capable of developing adequate vacuum for the booster to function properly. A severely worn engine, a vacuum leak, or a high-performance engine with a modified camshaft may not have the vacuum needed for acceptable assist. Aftermarket electric vacuum pumps are available. Some diesel trucks use a mechanical vacuum pump to provide more vacuum.

When the brake pedal is depressed, the internal spool valve in the power booster slides and opens and closes ports to regulate the pressure and vacuum for assist. If the vehicle is pulling a heavy load, adequate vacuum may not be available for braking. For this reason, many heavy-duty trucks use hydroboost brake assist.

The manifold vacuum of an engine is at its highest when at idle or the vehicle is decelerating. This is why the vacuum booster is so effective. If a vacuum leak occurs or the engine cannot develop adequate vacuum due to engine wear or performance modifications, the brake assist may not be adequate. Pull the vacuum hose and check for vacuum with the engine running and check to be sure that the one-way check valve in the master cylinder is okay. It should allow flow in one direction but not the other.

The system might malfunction if engine vacuum is low due to engine mechanical problems. If in doubt, use a vacuum gauge to check for engine vacuum while the engine is idling at normal operating temperature. It should be around 20 inches (naturally aspirated gasoline engines only).

System Diagnosis

A leaking diaphragm causes a hissing noise under the instrument panel that may change its tone when the brakes are applied. This is an indication of booster failure. If the booster is leaking severely, a rough idle may be detected or positive fuel trims may be present on a scan tool.

The proper way to test a vacuum booster is to pump the brakes several times with the engine off and then hold the pedal while you start the engine. The pedal should drop slightly when the engine starts. If it does not drop, the booster or vacuum source likely has a problem. When the booster fails, a hard, high brake pedal is usually present. The vehicle is difficult to stop due to the pedal force requirements. The diaphragm is not using vacuum and atmospheric pressure to help you stop. There

could be a hole in the diaphragm or a problem with the valving inside the unit. In either case, the entire booster must be replaced.

Sometimes, the master cylinder develops an external fluid leak into the booster and both components must be replaced. In severe cases, an unexplained loss of brake fluid can be traced to the fluid being drawn into the booster from a leaking O-ring where the master cylinder and booster bolt together. Over time the brake fluid inside the booster can cause damage and then be pulled into the intake manifold through the check valve and hose.

Any brake fluid found inside the large vacuum hose between the vacuum booster and the intake manifold means that the booster and master cylinder must be replaced. This condition can even cause the vehicle to

If brake fluid is found running down the power booster under the master cylinder (arrow) it could mean that the external O-ring in the master cylinder has allowed brake fluid to enter the power booster and damage it. In this case, the master cylinder and booster should be replaced. Be sure that what you are seeing is not just a spill from overfilling the master cylinder.

The brake pedal linkage needs to be disconnected from the power booster. A clevis pin through the hole (arrow) is secured by a clip. The four studs visible here go through the firewall and are secured by nuts that are accessible from under the dash. Needle-nosed pliers can be used to remove the clip from the rod. The four nuts under the dash are normally accessible.

have smoke at the tailpipe because the engine is literally burning the brake fluid.

System Repair

The booster can be replaced separately or with the master cylinder if both have failed. Booster replacement is generally straightforward. In most cases, the master cylinder can be removed from the booster by removing two nuts (most using a deep 15-mm socket) and leaving the metal brake lines attached. Carefully move the master cylinder forward, slightly flexing the lines to allow enough room for the booster to be removed from the bulkhead (firewall). On some models, the lines may need to be removed to avoid damaging them. Cap them with rubber caps or rubber hoses plugged with a bolt.

The booster is attached to the bulkhead by four nuts under the instrument panel. The rod to the brake pedal must also be disconnected. A pin and washers are usually used to attach the rod to the pedal lever, which can be removed with needle-nosed pliers.

To install the replacement unit, reverse the removal procedure and be sure to properly bleed the brakes if the lines were disconnected from the master cylinder. If brake pedal height requires adjustment, follow the service information for your vehicle.

Hydroboost

Hydroboost provides assist on vehicles with low manifold vacuum or where adequate space is not available for a vacuum booster. Supercharged or turbocharged engines may also use a hydroboost unit because of increased pressure in the induction system. Diesel engines do not use a conventional throttle plate and therefore do not develop intake manifold vacuum like a gasoline engine. They also may use hydroboost assist or an engine-driven or

When replacing a booster, it is sometimes possible to leave the master cylinder attached to the brake lines and support it with wire out of the way. This saves time by not having to bleed the brakes after booster replacement.

electric vacuum pump with a vacuum booster. Some heavy-duty trucks may not have adequate vacuum under high loads, such as when towing on mountain roads, so hydroboost is used in these applications as well.

In hydroboost systems, power steering fluid under pressure is used inside of a piston chamber to increase the force on the master cylinder input rod.

How It Works

The hydroboost unit is also mounted on the bulkhead (firewall) with the master cylinder bolted to one side and the brake pedal linkage attached to the other side. Mounting is similar to the vacuum booster design.

In most applications, a high pressure power steering hose supplies fluid from the power steering pump to the hydroboost unit. Another hose leads from the hydroboost unit to the power steering gear. Additional low pressure hoses return the fluid back to the power steering pump or remote reservoir.

When the brake pedal is applied with the engine running, a sliding spool valve inside the hydroboost unit moves and high pressure fluid is supplied to a "power" piston, which is mounted around the rod from the brake pedal to the master cylinder. The pressurized fluid increases the force on the master cylinder, which provides the brake assist. An internal fluid passage on the spool valve inside the hydroboost unit allows constant fluid flow to the power steering pump so that assisted steering is always available regardless of brake pedal position.

A high-pressure accumulator (HPA) on or inside the hydroboost unit stores pressurized power steering fluid as a failsafe in the event that the engine would die or power steering pump pressure is not available. It uses a high strength spring or a dry nitrogen charge inside of a chamber with a rubber diaphragm or sealed piston.

When the engine starts, high pressure power steering fluid against the diaphragm or piston compresses the high strength spring or the nitrogen charge in the accumulator chamber. This chamber of high-pressure power steering fluid is routed to the power piston for assist as a backup or failsafe in the event of power steering pump loss or engine failure for at least two assisted stops.

System Diagnosis

If the vehicle develops a high, hard brake pedal, but the power steering assist is normal, it is likely that the hydroboost unit is at fault. The symptoms are similar to vacuum booster failure. If the power steering also has little or no assist, the problem may be in the power steering pump or hoses.

To properly test a hydroboost system, pump the brake pedal several times with the engine off. Hold the pedal down and start the engine. The pedal should drop slightly and then "kick" back up if the system is functioning normally. Test drive the vehicle to verify proper brake performance at various speeds and engine RPM. Inspect the power steering drive belt and fluid level in the power steering pump. Verify that the power steering system works correctly.

Power steering leaks are not uncommon on the hoses or fittings or from the hydroboost unit itself.

Hydroboost brake assist uses power steering pressure to reduce brake pedal effort. As long as the engine is running, assist is available no matter what the engine load.

An HPA using a heavy spring or nitrogen is pressurized when the engine starts. This accumulator is a backup system in the event that the engine dies. It provides at least two assisted stops.

When testing a hydroboost system, pump the brakes several times and start the engine while holding the pedal. The pedal should drop and then kick back up if the system is working properly. A normal vacuum booster pedal should drop when the engine starts but not kick back up.

Removing a hydroboost unit is similar to the procedure for removing a vacuum booster. The main difference is that there are several lines attached to the hydroboost unit.

When the power steering level drops significantly, the power steering pump develops a whining sound when turning. This is often the first indication of a problem, but power steering fluid leakage is likely present under the vehicle.

System Service

Hydroboost replacement is similar to vacuum booster replacement except that the hydraulic lines need to be removed. Caution: If the system requires service, the accumulator must be depressurized prior to any work. Most applications require that the brake pedal be pressed multiple times to deplete the high pressure. (Consult factory service information for your vehicle for specific methods). You must not attempt to remove the accumulator or related attachment pins without following the factory procedures for removal. Most applications require that the entire assembly be replaced in the event of failure, so accumulator removal is not required at any time.

Before attempting to remove a hydroboost unit, place a pan under the vehicle to catch power steering fluid, which is sure to escape from the lines when they are disconnected. Depressurize the accumulator using your vehicle's factory service methods. The master cylinder must be removed from the hydroboost unit.

You may be able to leave the brake lines connected and flex them slightly as you move the master cylinder forward to allow room for hydroboost removal. If necessary, remove the brake lines from the master cylinder and cap them off to avoid fluid loss and possible contamination. You need to disconnect the hydraulic lines attached to the hydroboost unit at this time. Some applications may use the same-size threads on the fittings, so be sure to mark the position with tape or take a photo prior to removal so that you don't put the lines in the wrong ports. This will likely cause severe damage to the replacement unit or even the power steering gear.

The hydroboost unit is bolted to the bulkhead (firewall). Some applications require a deep 15-mm socket to remove the four nuts under the instrument panel. You also need to disconnect the brake pedal linkage prior to removing the hydroboost unit from the vehicle. Most applications use a spring clip and washer, which can be removed with needle-nosed pliers while you are under the dash.

Installation is the reverse of removal, but be sure to use new O-rings on the line fittings (if equipped). Torque all fasteners to manufacturer's specifications and be sure to properly attach the brake pedal linkage. Be sure to properly bleed the brakes if the lines were disconnected from the master cylinder. If brake pedal free play requires adjustment, follow the service information for your vehicle.

Power Steering Fluid Refilling on Hydroboost Systems

After all components are installed and the hoses connected, you need to refill the power steering system. Filling the power steering system fluid after hydroboost replacement

Reduce Pump Whine and Pulsation

Some Fords are prone to air intrusion, which can cause excessive pump whine and pulsation during hydroboost system refilling. Before starting the engine after refilling on a Ford system, you may want to use the procedure below. It helps reduce starting pressure, which reduces whine and pulsation when the engine is started.

1. Disable the engine to allow cranking without starting. On most vehicles, an easy way to disable the engine is to remove the fuel pump fuse or relay and relieve the fuel pressure by starting the engine.

2. Fill the reservoir with the correct power steering fluid. Crank the engine for 10 seconds while steering lock to lock with wheels off the ground. Caution: To avoid starter damage, do not crank the engine more than 15 seconds at a time.

3. Refill the pump reservoir as necessary and repeat the crank/refill procedure until the fluid level is correct. ∎

---

requires extra care so that air does not enter the system. Follow the factory service information.

Generally, the first step is to raise the front wheels off the ground using the appropriate safety practices including the use of jack stands and wheel chocks.

Fill the power steering fluid reservoir and turn the steering wheel completely to the left and right (without starting the engine) about 12 times. Refill the reservoir and continue turning the steering wheel back and forth until the fluid level no longer drops in the reservoir.

Now start the engine. With the engine running and the wheels off the ground, steer the vehicle left and right and top off the reservoir as needed. Check for leaks and then lower the vehicle and test drive.

Electronic

Many high-end and hybrid vehicles use electronic assist, which is a major departure from conventional brake assist. A brake pedal travel sensor is used to monitor driver input electronically. Some use a hydraulic pressure chamber similar to a miniature master cylinder with pressure transducers that measure pressure and convert it to electrical signals. This design produces a natural brake feel in the pedal for customer comfort. These electrical signals are sent to a brake modulator.

In other words, there is no conventional master cylinder sending brake fluid to each wheel. This is not a new concept and has been used on some German vehicles for more than 10 years. For more on this system, see chapter 9: ABS, ADAS, and Related Systems.

The Mercedes Sensatronic brake system generates extreme pressures and all safety precautions must be following when servicing this system. At engine start, the system is capable of pressures more than 2,000 psi.

Some manufacturers such as Mercedes Benz use an electric pump and accumulator to supply brake assist from a modulator instead of a conventional master cylinder and booster setup. This design has a pedal-feel simulator so that the brake pedal feels more normal.

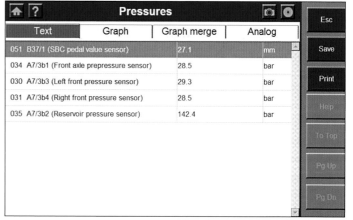

The Mercedes system develops very high pressure to apply the brakes directly from the Sensatronic brake module instead of the master cylinder. When servicing this system, follow the vehicle service information to avoid damaging the system and creating a safety hazard.

BRAKE SYSTEM TROUBLESHOOTING

First, be sure the problem isn't just worn-out brake pads!

Older cars had a lot of mass in the heavy cast-iron and steel parts used in the brake system, frame, and wheels. Fuel economy and emissions control were not at the top of engineers' lists back then, but now they are. Modern vehicles are designed to be lighter so that less fuel is used to reduce vehicle emissions and their effect on the atmosphere. Plastic, aluminum, and other lightweight materials have been substituted, which are not as good at absorbing vibration.

In the 1970s, you could slap a set of brake pads on the front of your Chevelle SS and pay little attention to anything else and you would likely get away with it, but not today. More care must be taken during a brake job to reduce the possibility of brake noise because the vibration is more likely due to less mass in the brake system.

Brake Noise

All brakes have vibration, causing noise. The trick for engineers is to be sure that the noise (brake squeal) is not audible to humans. Most people can hear in a range of 20–20,000 hertz. Mass helps to absorb noise, but newer vehicles have less mass, so other measures are taken to reduce the possibility of brake noise or squeal, which is one of the main reasons for comebacks after a brake job in a shop.

Older vehicles used cast-iron and steel components for the brake and suspension systems. These heavy components reduced the possibility of brake noise or squeal.

Today's vehicles are designed to increase fuel economy and reduce emissions, so they use lightweight components such as aluminum and plastic. Lighter weight brake and suspension components are not as good at absorbing vibration due to reduced mass. Brake noise and squeal is more common.

Cause: Worn, Damaged, or Missing Brake Hardware

Hardware should always be replaced and properly lubricated during a brake job. Heat can fatigue the hardware, which affects the way the pads are held in the caliper. Hardware that is worn, damaged, or bent is pretty easy to see, but the effect that excess heat causes is not always visible. During a brake job, since the brakes are apart and the cost is minimal, it makes sense to replace the hardware as a matter of course. Most professionals recommend hardware replacement with every brake job.

Be sure to use the right lubricants. Metal-to-metal contact points generally use anti-seize compound or special ultra-temp brake lubes. Never use common chassis grease or oil on brake systems. Rubber or synthetic rubber compounds must not be exposed to petroleum-based or anti-seize lubricants. The rubber used in brake systems can swell and the synthetic parts can bind, leading to noise, uneven pad wear, and other issues. Clear silicone brake lubricant in a tube is excellent for these areas.

Some disc brake lubricants come in a plastic bottle with a brush in the cap that can be used on both metal and rubber contact points. Most of these work well and are worth the cost if they come from a trusted supplier.

Most brake pads include a shim on the backside of the pad for noise reduction. This shim can wear away or fall off over time. If the pad used a shim from the factory, it is necessary to reinstall it.

Do not spray anything directly on the pad or rotor friction surface. Some products claim they can be used in this way to stop brake noise, but most are found to be nothing more than solvents that could cause damage to the binders that hold the friction material together and lead to inadequate braking. Unless the company that manufactured your vehicle endorses an additive or chemical, it is wise to stay away from it. Miracle cures for brake noise are generally ineffective and can cause damage to the system or affect system operation.

Brake engineers work hard to develop a friction formulation for the needs of their vehicles. Manufacturers may use several formulations depending on vehicle size, weight, and intended use to obtain good stopping, low dusting, reduced noise, and the longest possible service life.

Don't Mistake Silicone Gasket Sealer for Silicone Lubricant

I once suggested that silicone lube be used to lubricate the brake system caliper slides on a vehicle that a coworker was servicing at home. The coworker brought in the vehicle, very upset that his brakes were binding and the vehicle was pulling. Upon inspection, I found that the calipers were covered with orange RTV silicone gasket sealer!

Apparently, the coworker went to a local chain store and picked up a tube of RTV silicone gasket sealer and used it on all on his caliper slides and the back of the pads, causing major problems.

Do not mistake silicone gasket sealer for silicone lubricant. They are very different! ∎

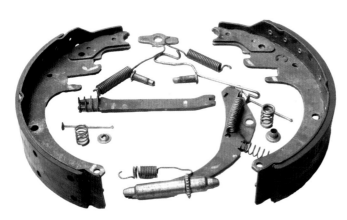

One way to reduce the possibility of brake noise is to use new brake hardware instead of the old parts. The original parts may look fine, but it is hard to determine if a spring has lost some of its temper and may not be able to control vibration as it should.

It is also important to use the proper lubricant on the components. Do not use any petroleum-based lubricant on rubber or synthetic brake components. Specific brake lubricants are available that work well and are relatively inexpensive. Most are silicone based so that they do not attack rubber parts.

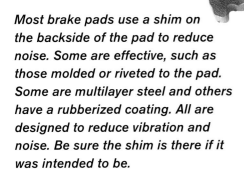

Most brake pads use a shim on the backside of the pad to reduce noise. Some are effective, such as those molded or riveted to the pad. Some are multilayer steel and others have a rubberized coating. All are designed to reduce vibration and noise. Be sure the shim is there if it was intended to be.

Some brake pads are designed differently than the OEM pad with chamfers, slots, or even multiple friction surfaces. This is an attempt to break up the vibration and eliminate noise. It is wise to stick with a name-brand supplier to reduce noise and provide optimal brake performance.

It is wise to stick with the type of friction formulation for the original equipment pads. For example, if a formulation with less metallic content than the original equipment pad is used on a one-ton truck pulling a horse trailer, the vehicle may not stop as well due to the change in coefficient of friction (COF).

Many light trucks and SUVs are equipped with semimetallic pads. Pads with an even higher percentage of metallic content are available and intended for severe duty, such as racing, ambulance, police, and heavy-duty trucks. These are called carbon-metallic pads and require hotter rotor surfaces to properly function. Therefore they would not be a good choice for a lightweight passenger car that does not develop high rotor temperatures.

Many automotive applications call for ceramic or organic pads. The pad construction and friction formulations have a big effect on noise.

Cause: Excessive Heat or Dust

Heat and dust are factors that can add to noise creation. If aftermarket wheels are installed or shields are placed between the rotor and the wheel to reduce brake dust on the rims, it could play a part in brake performance, pad life, and noise production. Many rotors are now produced overseas and not all have the same metallurgy, mass, and surface finish as the OEM rotor did. This can also lead to the production of brake noise and higher pedal force requirements.

Cause: Poor Rotor Surface

Whether you have the rotors turned or buy new ones, their surface must be smooth enough to provide good contact with the new pads to adequately stop. The force required may be higher until brake use causes the pads to "bed in" or burnish. This is a process by which the two surfaces wear against each other until they become smoother and achieve almost complete surface contact with each other while braking.

If the newly machined or replacement rotor has an excessively rough surface, a high roughness average (RA), the pads can vibrate when applied and squeal. Higher pedal force and more brake dust on the wheels may also occur. Be sure that your rotors are as smooth as possible when they are installed and that you properly "break in" the new pads when driving after the new brake job. See chapter 3: Disc Brake Systems for the proper method.

The trick to noise control is to use quality parts, new hardware, the proper lubricant in the right places, and machine the rotors and drums very smooth but not below specs. The more metal you remove, the more heat is generated. The less mass you have, the more the rotors tend to vibrate in an audible range to humans.

If you have to buy new rotors, stick with well-known, respected

Select Quality Over Price

Don't base your pad choice on price or low dusting. Stick with the same type of pad the vehicle manufacturer used and buy a name brand that has a track record of quality. The shim material on the back of the pad is also important. It can be multilayer steel, rubber coated, or even friction material. The squeeze container of blue goo that comes with some pads is probably the least effective but better than nothing on the back of the pads to help control noise.

Some aftermarket designs use different friction shapes, chamfers, and slots to break up the harmonics across the pad and reduce vibration and noise. One manufacturer uses a laser vibrometer to analyze pad noise at different areas of the pad on a dynamometer and then chamfers the pad edges to reduce vibration and noise. Some pads even have separate pad sections that look quite different than the OEM pad. ∎

Some aftermarket rotors do not have the same mass or surface finish that the OE rotor had. This may affect noise levels and brake performance, especially right after the brake job. A rougher surface usually results in higher pedal effort until the friction and rotor surface smooth out and "burnish" to each other. It is a good idea to replace rotors in pairs.

When a rotor is machined, it must be within thickness specifications to provide safety and heat control. The surface must be smooth enough to provide good surface contact between the rotor and pads. A rough surface can cause more noise due to vibration.

This drum brake backing plate has six shoe support pads that the shoes slide on when they are applied and released. Over time, grooves can develop, which the shoes can catch on as they move, creating a popping noise as the brakes are applied and released. Here, you can see a groove worn in the shoe support in the upper right (arrow).

manufacturers. Some overseas suppliers have poor surface finishes and the metallurgy does not match the OEM in terms of quality gray iron (what rotors and drums are made from).

Another key point is how you treat the brakes after you finish the job. Proper break in (burnishing) of the fresh brake job is just as important as how you break-in a new engine. Take it easy and do several light to moderate stops with a cool-down period between each one so that the friction and rotor or drum surface can mate together and achieve good surface contact. This results in efficient, quiet, and long-lasting brake service.

Popping Sound When Braking

If the noise is coming from the rear, check for grooves worn in the shoe support pads where the brake shoes rest against the backing plates. High-mileage vehicles often develop wear grooves that the shoes get caught in when applying and releasing. It might be possible to weld and

file these support pads, but backing plate replacement may be required. Be sure to lube each of the support pads during a drum brake job. There are usually six of them, three behind each shoe.

Worn, damaged, or fatigued hold-down springs could also be the culprit. Look at the drum surface to be sure it is not grooved.

Too coarse of a cut on a brake lathe produces a spiral groove that the shoes try to follow when braking. This could also cause shoe movement and noise. This can also occur on a rotor that has too coarse of a cut on the lathe.

If the noise is coming from

the front, take a good look at the rotor finish. If the rotor surface has grooves that look like a record album (remember those?), the pad will try to move with the grooves and pop or rattle when it contacts the surface.

Brake Grinding

A grinding noise when braking is usually caused by metal-to-metal contact due to severely worn pads or shoes or a hardware failure due to improper assembly allowing parts to drop into the drum. Grinding from a disc brake can also be due to severely worn pads or a shim coming loose and contacting the rotor.

Brake Pull

If the vehicle pulls to one side when the brakes are applied, several things must be checked. A restricted brake hose or crushed line reduces the brake fluid flow to one side and the vehicle can pull in the other direction. If you suspect a hose restriction, pump up the pedal, release the brake, and then see if you can turn the wheel. If the wheel is locked with the pedal released, open the brake bleeder. If fluid squirts out and the wheel turns free, you have a restriction between the caliper and the master cylinder.

A loose wheel bearing also causes a pull in the other direction. On disc brakes, it could be accompanied by a low pedal because the piston may be pushed back by the angle of the rotor. As the pedal is depressed, the rotor must become vertical before the brakes can apply, causing a lower-than-normal pedal.

A stuck caliper piston or rusted caliper slide can have the same effect. If a caliper is causing brake drag, the vehicle can pull in that direction with the brakes released.

Replacing pads or a rotor on one side only can also cause a brake pull because the surfaces have a different coefficient of friction than the other side.

Contaminated friction surfaces also affect braking. Oddly enough, the side with the contamination usually grabs due to the heat making the liquid become sticky like glue rather than slippery. Contaminated friction material usually causes that wheel to grab and lock up faster than usual.

A major suspension problem, such as a bent strut or shock, damaged spring, bound-up ball joint, or alignment issue, can also cause a pull in one direction. Check the tires for correct pressure and size. If the vehicle pulls without the brakes applied but are okay when applied, check the tires, power steering, and alignment. For best results, all tires should be the same size and brand and have the same amount of wear. If too great a variation exists, a constant pull or a pull during braking can result.

Nosedive

A vehicle can develop an unusual front end drop during braking, which is known as nosedive. The common cause for this condition is that the rear brakes are not functioning. When the rear brakes are not working, the rear rotors or drums have an unusual amount of rust on the friction surface. This is an indication that the pads or shoes are not making adequate contact when braking.

Check for a restricted hydraulic line or hose to the rear, a stuck combination valve, or a malfunctioning ABS unit. Lines can become crushed during vehicle repairs when the vehi-

If a rotor or drum has a heavy rust coating, it is likely that the brake is not working. Light surface rust is normal, especially in the morning in high-humidity climates. Raise the vehicle and have an assistant apply the brakes while you attempt to turn the wheel. If the rear rotors have rust and the fronts do not, it is likely that the front brakes will wear excessively because the rears are not doing their part.

cle is lifted on a hoist or jack. A hose can develop a restriction especially under a bracket in high-rust areas. A condition known as "rust jacking" can restrict the hose as the rust inside the bracket grows over time.

A stuck-open metering valve on a disc and drum system can cause nosedive on initial braking because the valve is designed to momentarily hold back fluid to the front brakes so that the rears can apply. A stuck-closed proportioning valve could also cause nosedive because fluid is able to get to the rear wheels. A stuck solenoid in the ABS modulator could also restrict fluid to the rear wheels. In this case, a code is likely stored in the ABS module and the ABS light may be on.

If different-size tires are used on a vehicle, front-to-rear brake balance may be affected.

Brake Pull Can Be the Result of a Major Issue

I once encountered a vehicle with a severe front brake pull. Upon inspection, it was discovered that one of the metal brake shims had come loose from one of the pads and was laying on top of the rotor hat. Over time, the shim cut completely through the hat like a lathe and cut the hat in two. This caused the friction surface on the rotor to separate from the hat and remain stationary. In other words, there was no braking on that wheel because the rotor was cut in two. ■

Brake Lockup

If the rear brakes lock up on a vehicle with rear drum brakes, be sure that the brakes are not adjusted too tight and the parking brake cables are free and are fully released.

Some applications have a bracket on the brake hose that can rust and choke the flow of fluid through the hose. This is known as rust jacking. To diagnose, apply the brakes and open the bleeder. If no fluid flows, crack the metal line connection at the hose. If fluid flows there but not at the bleeder, loosen the banjo bolt. If no fluid flows from there, the hose is restricted.

If brake fluid or gear lube gets on the brake shoes they lock up when the brakes are applied. Saturated shoes should be replaced and never cleaned. You also need to repair the source of the leak so that the problem does not reoccur.

Another reason for lockup is contaminated brake shoes. If rust or dirt is between the brake shoes and drum surface, braking can be affected. If a rear axle seal leaks grease onto the drum surface or a wheel cylinder leaks brake fluid, it can soak into the shoes and cause brake grab and lockup. It would seem that grease or brake fluid would act as a lubricant and keep the brakes from holding, but they actually lock up because the heat during braking from friction turns the fluid into a sticky substance on the shoes.

If the rears lock up under heavy stops, there could be a problem with a stuck-open proportioning valve or a stuck-closed metering valve. A brake line could be crushed or a hose kinked or restricted.

Pressure test gauges are available that attach to the brake bleeders, making it easy to check and compare pressures, but they are expensive for home use. The vehicle may have to be taken to a specialty shop that has hydraulic pressure gauges for advanced-level diagnosis.

Hard Pedal

If the brake pedal is abnormally hard and high and the vehicle is difficult to stop, check the operation of the vacuum brake booster. A bad booster or kinked or cracked vacuum hose can cause this condition. To test

A hard, high brake pedal is caused by a defective brake booster or vacuum problem. A hissing noise under the dash is another indication of booster failure. Be sure that the engine has enough vacuum at idle to supply the booster.

the booster, pump the brake pedal several times with the engine off and then start the engine with your foot firmly on the pedal. When the engine starts, the pedal should drop slightly. If a loud hissing sound is heard from under the dashboard that changes when you apply the brakes, the booster may have an external leak.

Another possible cause of a hard pedal is a lack of adequate engine vacuum. A vacuum leak, poor tuning, or engine wear/damage can cause low vacuum. Also, high-performance engines with aftermarket camshafts frequently produce low engine vacuum. Vacuum reservoirs or vacuum pumps are commonly used in high-performance applications.

Soft, Spongy, Sinking, or Low Pedal

A soft, spongy brake pedal that doesn't go to the floor means that air

A low brake pedal occurs if drum brakes are adjusted too loose, but the brakes could lock up if they are adjusted too tight. Binding parking brake cables can also cause the rear brakes to lock up or drag.

A high-performance engine may use a modified camshaft, which can reduce manifold vacuum and brake performance. A vacuum leak or other engine problem related to timing or wear can also reduce the vacuum needed to give good brake assist.

Check the vacuum with a vacuum gauge if you are encountering a hard pedal or have difficulty stopping. You may also have a defective booster or a crimped hose leading to it. The check valve allows flow only in one direction and can be checked by blowing through it in both directions.

is present in the hydraulic system. Check the fluid level in the master cylinder reservoir. If it is full, brake bleeding may be required. If you can "pump up" the pedal so that it is higher and firmer, the problem is likely air in the system. This must be removed by bleeding the brake system.

If the pedal goes completely to the floor and you have little or no braking, you may have a serious leak in the system. Get off the road as soon as you can safely do so and stop the vehicle. Look underneath for evidence of a leak and check the level in the master cylinder. The most common reason for this is a rusted brake line or bad hose that blew open. You might be able to nurse the car home in low gear using the parking brake, but a leak may require that your vehicle be towed home due to safety concerns. Don't risk an accident or getting someone hurt.

If you know that there are no leaks, but you have trouble getting a pedal at all, you can diagnose the problem by disconnecting the lines at the master cylinder. Plug them with block-off plugs (kits are available from tool sources) and step on the brake. If the pedal is okay now, you know the master cylinder is okay.

Next, install one line to see if the pedal remains firm. If it does,

the problem is in the circuit that is disconnected. Reattach it and work your way down the system, blocking off the fluid until you locate the problem. For example, if you block the lines going into the ABS unit and the pedal is good and then reattach them and block the lines coming out of the ABS unit and lose the pedal, the problem is air or some other problem inside the ABS unit. Sometimes a scan tool is needed to properly bleed an ABS unit.

If the pedal is low but hard, the rear brake shoes may need adjustment.

An ABS issue can also cause a soft, low pedal. Dirt in an ABS release valve is the common culprit if the ABS is at fault. The noticeable difference when a release valve is stuck

A brake pedal that goes to the floor or is low could be the result of a leak or a defective master cylinder. You may also have air in the hydraulic system or severely misadjusted rear brake shoes.

open is that the pedal eventually becomes firm and the vehicle stops before the pedal goes to the floor.

Another reason for a soft, sinking pedal can be a problem within the

If the pedal creeps slowly to the floor, especially under light pedal effort and the reservoir is full, the problem is usually a defective master cylinder. This condition is known as internal bypassing. A cup seal can split or wear in the area of the vent port, causing this condition. One way to eliminate any other possibility is to remove the brake lines at the master cylinder and plug them with fittings and then apply the brake. If the pedal acts the same, the master cylinder is bypassing.

A low brake pedal can also be caused by dirt stuck in the ABS unit. If the release valve is held open by a dirt particle, the fluid flows into the low-pressure accumulator (LPA) every time the brake pedal is depressed. This can easily be misdiagnosed as a master cylinder issue because the fluid level has not dropped. One cause of this is pushing back the caliper pistons without opening the brake bleeder valves. This allows dirty fluid to travel through the ABS unit as it travels back to the master cylinder.

master cylinder. If a torn cup seal is present inside the master cylinder, the pedal sometimes creeps to the floor at a stoplight and the vehicle starts to move forward. This is known as internal bypassing. If the pedal is pumped up or higher pedal force is used, the damaged cup seal may expand and seal momentarily, causing the brakes to hold. This condition often starts intermittently and degrades over time. The master cylinder must be replaced if this condition exists.

Pulsating Pedal and Steering Wheel Shimmy

The most common reason for brake pedal pulsation or steering wheel shimmy when braking is an excessive variation in the thickness of the rotors, causing the caliper pistons to move in and out as the rotor turns within the pads. This movement feeds back to the master cylinder and the brake pedal can move up and down as a result. Excessive rotor runout can also cause this condition if the caliper slides are binding.

Steering wheel shimmy (left-to-right movement when braking) can be intermittent because the rotors on each side of the vehicle can

be "in sync" or "out of sync" with each other as you go around turns. In other words, if the "high spots" on each rotor are in the same place side to side, the vehicle would have a pulsation, but the steering wheel may not. If the high spots become out of sync, the pulsation may be more evident in the steering wheel during that time.

Engineers will tell you that runout is the main cause of rotor thickness variation (also known as variation in parallelism). Thickness variation can often be felt in the pedal if it exceeds just 0.0005 inch. A common runout spec is 0.003 inch, but many manufacturers only allow 0.0005-inch thickness variation. To check runout, a dial indicator is used. A micrometer that reads in ten-thousandths of an inch is

needed to check for thickness variation. Because you likely do not have these special tools at home, you may choose to have your rotors turned or replace them during a brake job to eliminate the possibility of them being out of specification.

Some technicians feel that running through a puddle can cause runout issues when the water hits a hot rotor, but engineers don't agree. Temperatures must be much higher for the cast iron to deform in this way. Most runout and thickness variation issues result from poor rotor metallurgy or design or uneven torquing of the fasteners on the wheels.

Brake pedal pulsation can be caused by rotor thickness variation, excessive runout, or a drum that is egg shaped. If your vehicle is a disc-and-drum system, apply the parking brakes lightly while driving. If the vehicle pulsates, the drums are the problem.

Uneven lug-nut torque can cause rotor issues and brake pulsation. Be sure to torque the wheels in a star pattern to the proper specification. Do not use an impact wrench on the lug nuts without using a torque-limiting extension bar (commonly known as a "torque stick"). The torque stick should have a value that is lower than the torque specification. Finish tightening with a good torque wrench.

The metallurgy in a rotor is important to long-term performance and heat handling. Some aftermarket rotors have much less mass than the OEM rotor, which can cause many issues.

Brake Fade

A condition known as brake fade can occur when the brakes become hot. Less effective braking is the result. Drum brakes are more subject to fade than disc brakes because the heat can make the drum expand. The result is a fading or a lower-than-normal pedal because the shoes have to extend more to contact the larger diameter drum surface. Fade is not as common with disc brakes because heat causes the rotor to expand and that does not cause a low pedal.

Other types of fade that are less common are water fade, friction fade, gas, and particle fade. Water fade reduces friction inside the drum when driving in hard rain. The fade is more of an inability to stop as quickly until the water is expelled or dries from the heat. It is not common on disc brakes because they act as a natural squeegee to remove water on the surface of the rotor.

Friction (or lining) fade can occur from severely overheated pads or shoes. The internal adhesives can rise to the surface of the friction material and reduce its ability to grab onto the drum or rotor. This is referred to as a reduction in the coefficient of friction. Disc brakes can shed heat better than drums since drum brakes contain the heat within the drum during severe braking.

Gas or particle fade can occur when the friction material, rotor, or drum sheds particles that ride between the two surfaces. This is similar to the "marbles" that build up at the top of a NASCAR track during the race from tire wear. When a car drives into the "marbles," it usually ends up in the wall. Gases can also emit from the friction material that can affect the coefficient of friction but this is not very common. Higher pedal effort is required to maintain stopping power when this occurs. In racing, many teams use rotors with slots to release gases and wear particles. Smaller tracks, such as Martinsville, often cause brakes to run so hot that the rotors are glowing orange. This can be seen during the race through the wheels as the cars approach the turns.

Brake Drag, Smell, or Smoke

Overheating the brakes on a mountain road, excessive loading, or aggressive driving can create a burning smell from the brakes. A brand-new brake job can also cause a brake odor as the new friction material seats to the rotor surface.

A dragging caliper from dirt or rust or a binding parking brake cable can also cause overheating and a brake smell. Be sure that the brakes are not adjusted too tight.

Restricted hoses or crushed lines can cause brakes to drag. If this is suspected, open a bleeder. If the wheels turn free, look for a restriction going to that wheel. Incorrect fluid can cause internal swelling in the system and the brakes can drag or lock on after being applied.

Sometimes replacement rotors from overseas have a wax or oily coating inside the cooling fins to reduce rust. As the rotors heat up during braking, a smell or smoke can occur. This is often mistaken for a problem with the new brake pads. It is difficult to remove from the cooling fins and might have to just "burn" out as the brakes are used.

Low Fluid in the Master Cylinder

If the fluid level in the master cylinder drops over time on a vehicle with disc brakes, it is a normal condition. This occurs because the pistons must move out to make up for the reducing thickness of the brake pads as they wear. Thus, a low fluid level can mean that it is time for a brake job on a vehicle with disc brakes. Drum brakes self-adjust mechanically, so the wheel cylinders don't need to adjust to wear and the fluid

Brake fade can result from overheating the brakes. Abusive driving causes excessive temperatures, which can damage all components of the brake system and even some surrounding parts. Do not subject your brakes to conditions they aren't designed for. This is an extreme example but excessive rotor heat can be damaging and reduce braking ability.

Low fluid level in the master cylinder could indicate a leak in the system. The most common leak points are rusted brake lines, blown wheel cylinders, and brake hose failure. The level may also be low due to brake pad wear. Check the pad thickness before topping off the master cylinder.

Rapid or excessive brake pad wear can be caused by aggressive driving or resting your left foot on the brake pedal while driving. It can also be caused by the rear brakes not working properly due to a kinked brake line, collapsed hose, or ABS issue. Delphi VI ABS systems can malfunction and cause the rear brakes to cease functioning. This causes rapid wear of the front brakes.

should not drop as much in the master cylinder as the shoes wear.

A leak obviously causes a low fluid level. If you see a loss of fluid and brake fluid under the vehicle, it must be repaired immediately. A blown wheel cylinder or caliper could be the cause, but all too often it is the result of rusted brake lines, which must be replaced. Most automotive fluids, such as coolant, power steering fluid, and transmission fluid should keep at a constant level. If the level drops, a leak is present and must be repaired. Engine oil and brake fluid, on the other hand, may require refilling due to brake pad wear and engine wear.

Rapid Pad Wear

If front brake pads don't last as long as expected, be sure that the rear brakes are working properly. Rusted friction surfaces on rear rotors or drums indicate that they are not working. Aggressive driving or keeping your left foot on the brake pedal when driving can also cause excessive brake wear. The choice of friction material should be the same composition as the OEM pads to ensure that they perform and last as long as expected. Purchase your parts from a trusted source rather than gambling on an unknown brand.

A misadjusted pushrod between the power booster and master cylinder causes the brakes to drag or lock on as the fluid heats and expands and can't return to the master cylinder reservoir when the brakes are released. To check for a misadjusted pushrod, remove the master cylinder reservoir cap or lid and have an assistant press lightly on the brake pedal. If you see turbulence in the fluid as soon as the pedal is applied, it is an indication that the pushrod length is okay and is not the issue causing brake drag.

A malfunctioning ABS system can also affect normal braking. On systems such as the Delphi VI, motorized gears are used for ABS function, and, in some cases, the gear that operates the rear brakes can fall off. This eliminates rear brake function. This condition should illuminate the ABS light and the RBWL. Nosedive and rapid front pad wear can occur if this condition is present.

Dirty Fluid

Darkening of the fluid over time is normal due to the tendency of brake fluid to absorb the black dye in rubber components. Color should not be the only criteria for judging fluid condition. Use a test strip to determine fluid age by copper content. Moisture is absorbed into the fluid over time, so be sure to keep the lid on the master cylinder reservoir and the cap on the brake fluid bottle as much as possible.

If any petroleum-based liquid, such as motor oil or power steering fluid, enters the brake system, damage occurs. All system components containing rubber must be replaced. This includes the master cylinder, brake valves, ABS unit, hoses, calipers, and wheel cylinders. Basically everything must be replaced except the metal lines and they must be flushed with clean brake fluid before the new parts are installed.

As brake fluid ages, it turns darker as it absorbs dyes from the rubber parts in the system. Often a membrane-like layer forms in the bottom of the master cylinder. Periodically flushing the brake system with fresh fluid ensures optimal brake performance. Refer to your vehicle manufacturer's recommendations for proper service intervals.

ABS, ADAS, *AND* RELATED SYSTEMS

Most newer vehicles use a conventional master cylinder with disc brakes at all four corners. Older models with disc and drum systems typically used mechanical controls for front-to-rear bias during harsh braking and to reduce nosedive. Over the years, many mechanical brake controls have been replaced by electronic module (computer) control. One of the first additions was the ABS (Antilock Brake System).

ABS has been around for years, but now it acts as the base system for many other electronic control systems, such as traction assist, stability control, and certain functions of ADAS (Advanced Driver Assist

Systems). A few manufacturers have replaced the traditional master cylinder with a pedal-travel sensor and use electronic control of a pressure modulator to apply the brakes.

Most electronic systems are reliable, but the sensors and related wiring and connectors can sometimes fail due to being in harsh environments under the vehicle where salt, moisture, dirt, heat, cold, and vibration are present. The module or modulator can malfunction, but that is not as common as sensor and related wiring issues.

For all the related systems to work as they were designed, the base brake system (pads, rotors, shoes, drums,

hydraulics, etc.) must work properly. This means that the proper coefficient of friction must be present so that the amount of braking applied during electronic control is what the chassis engineer intended. If it is not, the sensors may cause system shutdown and set trouble codes. For this reason, it is important to keep the system operating in the same ranges as the OEM parts did. This can be accomplished through quality work using quality parts.

The basic operation of the ABS system is pretty simple, but its presence is important to other systems that use individual brake control. The base brake system is the basis for

The modulator is the heart of the ABS system. It is mounted in the hydraulic lines between the master cylinder and the wheels and controls pressure to reduce wheel lockup and help maintain vehicle control. It can also be used during stability- and traction-control functions.

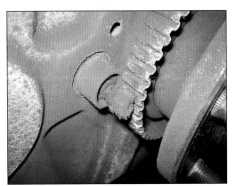

Many brake and chassis systems use sensors under the vehicle. They are subjected to contamination from water and salt and are also affected by vibration and heat cycling. These sensors are often the cause of an ABS warning lamp and a trouble code, but proper diagnosis should be performed before simply replacing the sensor.

ABS, and ABS is the base system for more advanced systems such as stability control, traction control, and ADAS. Future autonomous vehicles will still need the base brake system, even with the absence of steering wheels and brake pedals. It will likely be even more critical for flawless base brake operation when those vehicles become common on the street.

ABS Operation

Although experimental ABS systems were being developed in the early 1900s, the first actual use of ABS was on aircraft and trains. These systems were basic and generally just pulsed the brakes on and off similar to mechanically pumping the brake pedal with your foot (known as cadence braking). In the 1970s, several automotive manufacturers began to offer a more modern ABS systems using electronics. Many only affected the rear wheels, but some controlled all four wheels.

The first mainstream use of ABS in the domestic arena was on pickup trucks in the late 1980s. The systems had only one hydraulic channel and was manufactured by Kelsey-Hayes. It was known as Rear Wheel Antilock (RWAL) on General Motors- and Chrysler-built vehicles and Rear Antilock Brake System (RABS) on Fords. A handful of import manufacturers also used the Kelsey-Hayes system on the rear brakes of their pickups and vans. The system was eventually phased out and replaced with multiple-channel systems beginning in the mid-1990s. Most rear-wheel-drive vehicles now use three separate hydraulic channels, and most front-wheel-drive vehicles use four separate hydraulic channels.

One-Channel ABS

The Kelsey-Hayes RWAL/RABS system was pretty basic, using one sensor in the transmission tail shaft or rear differential and a simple computer known as an Electronic Brake Control Module (EBCM) to hold or reduce pressure through a single hydraulic line to the rear wheels. The intent was to eliminate rear wheel lockup and loss of control on lightweight pickup trucks and vans, especially in turns. This early ABS system, as basic as it was, reduced that possibility and reduced accidents. It was classified as a one-sensor, one-channel, two-wheel ABS system because it did not control the front wheels.

A main input to the EBCM is the brake switch signal, so if you have a vehicle with inoperative ABS, be sure that the brake pedal switch or sensor is functioning. Check to see if the brake lights work when the pedal is depressed, but keep in mind that some switches and sensors perform multiple functions and that brake light operation does not guarantee that the EBCM is receiving the signal. A scan tool might be needed to verify that.

All ABS systems use three modes during operation: hold, release, and reapply. On the single-sensor, single-channel version, the EBCM was programmed to monitor the deceleration rate of the single rear sensor because it did not have other sensors to compare speeds. A normal stop on dry pavement produced a sensor deceleration rate that was gradual (60, 59, 58, 57, etc.) and the computer did

One of the first light-vehicle ABS systems was used on pickup trucks and vans in the late 1980s and 1990s. It was a one-channel, one-sensor system designed to reduce rear-wheel lockup. It had its limitations, but all modern ABS systems evolved from the strategy of this early design.

One of the most important inputs to the ABS processor is the brake pedal input. Without it, the ABS does not function. The first step is to make sure that the brake lights work, but keep in mind that some systems use multi-pin brake pedal travel sensors rather than a simple ON/OFF switch and the brake lights can still function on a partially failed sensor.

The ABS module (arrow) reads inputs to control outputs just like any computer does. If the brake pedal is depressed and one wheel speed sensor looks different than the others, the ABS processor attempts to prevent lockup of the affected wheel by using three modes. It can HOLD pressure, RELEASE pressure, or REAPPLY pressure to the affected wheel(s).

Some models use a rear ABS sensor mounted in the differential housing (arrow). This design is known for early failure. If an ABS light is on, pull codes; if the rear ABS sensor is listed, check it for resistance. When it fails, it usually fails open, so your digital volt/ohm meter (DVOM) shows over limit (OL; high resistance) when testing between the sensor pins.

not actuate ABS operation when these conditions were present.

If the vehicle was on slippery pavement, such as a sheet of ice, the deceleration rate was more excessive (perhaps 60–0) when the wheels locked up and the computer actuated ABS operation by first going into the hold mode. The hold mode uses a solenoid controlling an isolation (or inlet) valve inside of a hydraulic modulator that is in series with the rear wheels. It is capable of blocking the fluid flow to the rear wheels so that the driver does not add additional pressure, making matters worse.

If the sensor signal from the rear wheels indicates that they are still locking up, the EBCM actuates the release mode. This is accomplished by another electric solenoid, which opens the release valve. This valve is also inside the hydraulic modulator and connected to the line leading to the rear wheels. When it opens, the hydraulic pressure trapped between the isolation valve and the rear wheels

can be vented to a low-pressure accumulator (LPA). When this occurs, the rear wheels release and start to rotate.

The LPA is nothing more than a piston in a bore with a lightweight spring behind it. Opening the release valve allows the pressure to reduce because it gives the fluid somewhere to escape inside the system. In heavy-duty truck air-brake systems, the same thing occurs during the release mode, but the air can be allowed to escape to the atmosphere. Engineers don't have that luxury with hydraulic brakes, so the LPA is used as a temporary storage container.

When the outlet valve is opened

and the brakes are released during the release mode, the affected wheel(s) ceases to lock up. The isolation valve reopens (reapply mode) and if the brakes begin to lock again the process repeats. The driver likely notices some brake pedal pulsations, which may cause some concern, but this is normal with early ABS systems.

Most systems are capable of multiple pulses per second. When the brake is released on vehicles with RWAL/RABS, the spring in the LPA returns the piston to its normal position, which returns the fluid to the master cylinder reservoir so that it is empty and ready for the next

Most ABS systems use two solenoids per circuit to hold or release fluid to an LPA. This is a single-channel system. The HOLD solenoid is on the left and the RELEASE solenoid is on the right. The brass piston on the right is the LPA. In the center is the white reset switch that monitors system operation.

If dirt holds the release valve open, the brake pedal is low. To test for a leaking release valve, stick a pocket screwdriver in the accumulator vent cap hole and have an assistant step on the pedal. Any movement indicates a leaking valve, requiring replacement of the modulator.

When an ABS malfunction occurs, most systems shut down and illuminate a yellow or amber ABS lamp on the instrument panel. When this occurs, the ABS module stores a trouble code that can be retrieved to aid in diagnosis. If the problem is severe, the system may also illuminate the RBWL.

ABS stop.

If dirt sticks in the release valve orifice, the pedal is low during normal braking because the accumulator fills every time the brake is applied. To test for this, insert a pocket screwdriver in the LPA cap after removing the rubber stopper and press on the brake pedal while stopped. If the screwdriver moves, the release valve is stuck open.

If the system malfunctions or the ABS warning lamp is on, the first thing to do is to flash out the codes. Ford- and Chrysler-built vehicles had a separate amber ABS lamp, but General Motors used the same RBWL that was used for hydraulic failure and to advise the driver that the parking brake was applied.

On General Motors vehicles to determine the cause of the RBWL, turn on the ignition and apply the parking brake. If the lamp becomes brighter, the problem is either a hydraulic issue, low fluid, or an ABS malfunction. The next step is

to check the fluid level in the reservoir and fill if necessary. Unplug the ground wire on the pressure differential switch of the combination valve. If the lamp goes off, you have a hydraulic problem. If the lamp stays on, you have an ABS issue and a code stored that you could flash out to aid in diagnosis.

On these early systems, flash-out codes are accessed by grounding a terminal in the 12-pin data link connector (DLC) on GM products (OBD-I prior to 1996) or grounding a coiled-up wire found under the dash on Fords and Chryslers. When the appropriate wire or terminal is

grounded and the ignition turned on, the ABS lamp flashes out the code.

Codes are limited and most codes are only two digits. Two flashes followed by a pause and four flashes was code 24. The flashes repeat and some are followed with a different code indicating the end of code output.

Most of the codes are hard codes but soft codes were used on the early Ford RABS system. If you turn off the key before you flash out the code and the problem wasn't present at the time, you lost the code.

Later Fords with RABS II had hard codes. This also known as a Keep Alive Memory (KAM) code. Sensor

Notice the toothed tone ring and sensor mounted to the steering knuckle. When front-wheel speed sensors were added, more emphasis was placed on the ABS system maintaining steering. Pulsing the front wheels during a panic stop helps the driver be able to steer the vehicle away from dangerous conditions.

Many pickup trucks use a four-wheel, three-channel, three-sensor system. The rear wheels are controlled together and the front wheels are controlled by separate hydraulic circuits in the ABS modulator. This unit is mounted under the vehicle and the lines are especially prone to rust and corrosion from road salt and moisture.

Pumping the brakes during a panic stop was common before ABS was invented. The idea is to allow the tire to roll somewhat instead of completely locking up to allow steering. With ABS during a panic stop, the pedal should be held firmly and the vehicle steered around obstructions.

failures were common on these systems, especially when mounted in the rear differential. An ohmmeter across the ABS sensor terminals generally indicates an open sensor when it fails. Most sensors read between 800 and 2,500 ohms.

As ABS was improved, it was added to the front wheels and the main focus became vehicle control, which gave you the ability to steer during panic stopping. Shorter stopping distances are another goal of the ABS brake engineer, but ABS cannot always reduce stopping distance. The most effective braking and least stopping distance is obtained when the tires are right on the verge of skidding. This is referred to as threshold braking. In contrast, a vehicle with all four wheels locked, skidding on dry pavement, takes longer to stop and is uncontrollable.

There is one condition where locked wheels may stop a vehicle faster. That is when the tires are locked in deep snow or gravel. The snow or gravel tends to build up in front of the locked wheel and reduces stopping

distance, but again, the vehicle is not able to be steered.

Without ABS, the wheels lock during a panic stop if the pedal is pressed too hard. No matter where the wheels are steered the vehicle continues to travel in the same path as prior to lockup. This is similar to the way a personal watercraft travels when the throttle is released. Without the ability to steer around obstructions, a crash may result. Professional drivers used threshold and cadence braking long before ABS brakes became mainstream.

Cadence braking is rapid pumping of the brake pedal to maintain steering ability. Modern ABS systems perform much faster than the average driver can respond to dangerous situations because they may not have the skills of a professional driver. Increased brake safety can be attributed largely to ABS becoming standard equipment on most vehicles on the road today. Stability-control systems were mandated by the US government on all vehicles 2012 and newer (weighing

less than 10,000 pounds GVW). These systems use ABS to perform their function, which makes ABS very common on modern vehicles.

Multi-Channel ABS

On most rear-wheel-drive vehicles, a three-sensor, three-channel, four-wheel ABS system is used. The EBCM monitors each front wheel with a separate sensor and controls that wheel with a separate hydraulic channel from the brake modulator. The modulator generally contains an isolation and release valve for each wheel and a hydraulic pump as well as LPAs and HPAs. The hold, release, and reapply modes are used, but generally an HPA and pump are used during the reapply mode instead of opening the isolation valve. This reduces pedal pulsation and puts the EBCM in charge of all system pressures during an ABS stop.

When working on this system the HPA must be depressurized by pumping the brake pedal multiple times or by using a scan tool.

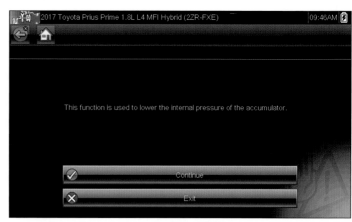

An HPA is used on many ABS systems to store pressurized fluid for the reapply mode. The pressure is very high and can cause serious injury. If service is required, follow service information guidelines.

To depressurize an accumulator, most manufacturers have a specific number of times that the brake pedal must be pumped to reduce the pressure to a safe level. Some use a scan tool to perform the process.

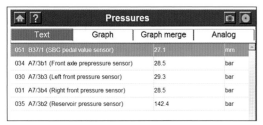

Here is an example of the extreme pressure inside of some modern brake systems. This scan tool screen capture came from a 2006 Mercedes E320 CDI with the Sensatronic brake system. This system is electronic and uses an HPA. 142.4 BAR is more than 2,000 psi.

Some Mercedes with electronic Sensatronic brake control have pressures as high as 2,000 psi. See service information for detailed information to avoid injury or damage to the system.

The rear wheels are monitored in the same way as the earlier RWAL/RABS system, using a sensor in the transmission tail shaft or the rear differential.

On most front-wheel-drive vehicles, a four-sensor, four-channel, four-wheel system is used, which means that each wheel has its own sensor and hydraulic channel.

ABS Sensors and Testing

The wheel speed sensors (WSS) are probably the most important part of the ABS system and when an ABS light is on, the most common failure is the sensors due to their location. The sensor can be mounted discretely, which means that you can see the toothed tone ring and sensor near the wheel or built into the bearing hub assembly, known as being integral.

Two types of signals are produced by sensors: analog and digital. Early sensors were analog (AC generating), which are two-wire sensors consisting of an iron core with a copper winding. When a metal bar is passed by this sensor, a magnetic field is generated. A ring consisting of many metal bars side by side, called the exciter or tone ring, spins with wheel speed; the WSS is placed very close to it.

The magnetic pulses generate an AC voltage (amplitude) as the wheel spins and each metal bar passes by with wheel rotation. Frequency (how fast the teeth pass by) is monitored to determine speed change, but the amplitude is also monitored by the ABS computer to determine proper operation. The system can even send a low-voltage signal to the sensors and back to determine if a short, or open, exists in the wiring before the vehicle even moves. This is called comprehensive monitoring.

Analog sensors are found on many current vehicles. They function well but are relatively slow. Because a computer only understands a digital (DC square wave) signal, the analog (AC) signal from the sensor must be converted to DC (digital) either inside the EBCM or by using another module between the sensor and the EBCM. If an external converter is used on GM vehicles, it is referred to as a digital ratio adapter controller (DRAC) or a vehicle speed signal (VSS) calibrator or buffer.

On many GM trucks and vans, this unit is located below the glove box and known to fail on some applications. When the vehicle has an ABS light on and inoperative speedometer and cruise control, replacement of the unit is often needed. If a front WSS code is generated on a Ford product, check to see if the tone ring is split and spinning on the outer CV joint.

When a wheel speed sensor (WSS) is not part of the bearing hub assembly, it is known as a discrete sensor (arrow). The air gap is generally not adjustable but can be affected by rust. If rust develops under the sensor bracket and changes its gap with the tone ring, unwanted ABS at low speeds is usually the result. This is known as rust jacking.

At times, an ABS sensor (tone) ring splits and freewheels on a front drive axle. This causes erratic signals and unwanted or no ABS on the affected wheel. It may not set a code. Visual inspection is always important when diagnosing an ABS issue. This particular issue sometimes occurs on Ford vehicles.

Because faster sensor speeds are necessary for stability control and other ADAS systems, newer vehicles are often equipped with DC sensors. They still have two wires and look the same as AC sensors. Although slightly more expensive, they produce a digital signal, which can be processed faster by the EBCM. An AC-to-DC converter is not required.

Digital sensors also function better at lower vehicle speeds and in reverse.

Another advantage is that the signal is not greatly affected by minor changes in the sensor air gap as it is with analog sensors. They do not generate AC voltage. They are actually supplied with battery voltage on one wire and return a low-DC (square wave) voltage signal back to the EBCM based on its wheel speed. The return voltage generally pulses between 0.8 and 1.65 volts as the wheel speed exciter ring teeth pass by. Some sensors actually

pulse the 12-volt input signal to monitor speed instead.

Analog and Digital Sensor Scan Tool Testing

A scan tool can be plugged into the data link connector (DLC) under the instrument panel to the left of the steering wheel near the driver's kick panel.

If the ABS lamp is on, a code should be present in history, and it

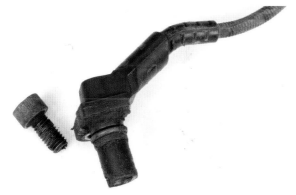

Here is a close-up of a discrete WSS using an O-ring and flange bolt for retention. It is common for the sensor to break when removed due to rust around it. It is also common for rust to develop under the sensor and "jack" it up, affecting gap and causing unwanted ABS operation on that wheel at low speeds.

This is an integral hub with an internal tone ring but with a removable sensor. This setup is common on GM-built pickups and SUVs. The sensor frequently breaks when removed, and the mounting hole requires cleaning before the new sensor can be installed.

When the ABS lamp illuminates, most vehicles shut down the ABS and store a code in memory. Late-model vehicles require a scan tool to retrieve the code. Plug a scan tool into the 16-pin connector (1996-up) to access the codes and data. They assist you in determining the nature of the malfunction. Many ABS failures are related to sensor malfunctions.

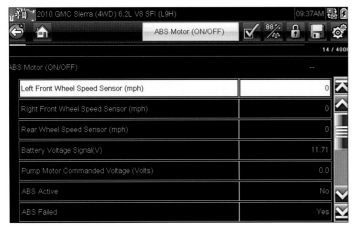

This data is available on the scan tool to determine WSS function. The vehicle can be driven and an assistant can view each wheel speed sensor's output to determine if they are functioning correctly. The scan tool can also command ON/OFF functions or warning lamps, the ABS motor, and solenoids.

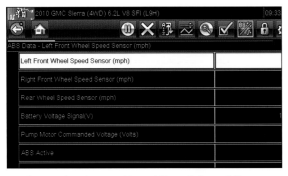

This scan tool screen shows the ABS data in digital form. Data such as wheel speeds and the status of the pump motor and solenoids are available. Using digital data is helpful, but it rapidly changes as the vehicle is driven. A glitch or intermittent drop-out may not be seen in this mode. In this screen capture, the vehicle was operated on a lift with the rear wheels spinning and the front wheels stopped.

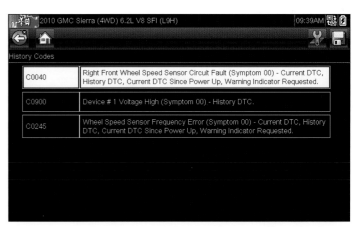

Here is an example of three codes found in an ABS module. Some codes are current and some are shown in history. Do not clear any codes until you have viewed service information on the procedures to follow.

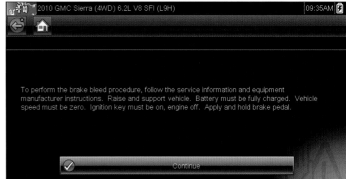

Here is the ABS automated bleed function. The scan tool can command the ABS system to power up the ABS pump and open the internal solenoids in a sequence to remove internal air that may have entered during service or a total loss of fluid due to a catastrophic leak.

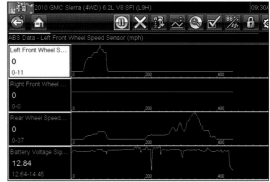

A more usable way to view the data on a scan tool is to use graphing. As you drive, the wheel speed sensors can be displayed on a graph, making it easier to see if one sensor has an intermittent issue (drop out). A scan tool can also command the motor or solenoids to operate. Automated bleed mode can help rid the unit of air.

Save Time by Reading Service Information

The owner of a 2001 Chevrolet K2500HD truck noticed that the ABS light was illuminated and obtained a scan tool to pull codes. The vehicle has an analog AC voltage-generating sensor. A left-front wheel sensor code was current, so he checked for proper resistance and AC voltage from the sensor. Neither were in specification, so he installed a new WSS in the hub. The old one broke coming out due to rust. This is fairly common, so he used a rotary brush to clean out the small hole where the sensor mounted.

He drove the vehicle only to find that the ABS light was still on. This time, the sensor was within resistance specs, but the AC voltage was low when spinning the wheel compared to the other side. He installed a new bearing hub because the tone ring is part of it. The AC output greatly improved, but the light stayed on when turning on the ignition. He continued to check wiring and connectors and then learned from service information that the vehicle must be driven to turn out the light.

After a short drive, the light went out and never came back on. Lesson learned: Save time by reading the service information and find out how the system works. ∎

could be current. It gives you some direction as to where the problem might be. It could be an issue with the solenoid, a switch, a motor, or an accumulator. The processor could have a power or ground concern or a sensor could have failed. The sensor is by far the most common culprit.

Wheel speed sensors are the most common failure points on ABS systems, but just because a code is present for a sensor does not mean it is the sensor itself. The attached wiring or connector could be at fault or the tone ring may have an issue. Vehicle data can be accessed while driving the vehicle to compare WSS speeds at each wheel. If the sensor has completely failed, it is easy to see that it is not generating a speed signal on the scan tool for that wheel, but some sensors may be operating marginally. When this occurs, you need to test the sensor at the wheel with a digital volt/ohm meter (DVOM) or a lab scope. A scan tool can display data digitally or in graph form. For intermittent problems, graphing the data is much more effective.

Other Uses of the Scan Tool with ABS

The scan tool can read ABS-related data in addition to displaying current and history codes. If a wheel is going into ABS prematurely, the scan tool can help determine which wheel is affected by watching the data for the solenoids on each wheel when ABS engagement occurs. The affected wheel shows activity on the scan tool and the others do not.

The scan tool can also perform automated bleed functions to remove trapped air from the ABS modulator and command certain components on and off. This can come in handy when diagnosing a difficult ABS problem.

Analog Sensor DVOM Testing

The first thing to do after safely raising the affected wheel is to unplug the connector leading to the WSS. Insert a Tee pin on the backside of each of the two wire connections close to the wire on the connector leading to the WSS (not the connector leading back to the EBCM). This is known as back probing and does not damage the connector.

Attach alligator clips to each Tee pin and connect them to the red and black leads on the DVOM. Place the DVOM control in "ohms" and read the value. A normal amount of resistance (ohms reading) for an analog sensor is 800–2,500 ohms. Most sensors fail "open," which means that the meter reads over limit (OL) when an open is present.

An open circuit is infinite resistance and a closed circuit is virtually no resistance. If you don't have specs readily available, you can compare the resistance to the other wheel speed sensors on the vehicle.

To diagnose a WSS, use Tee pins in the connector. These are available from department stores in the sewing department for drapery. They are large enough diameter to fit into the connector but not too big to fit under the Weather-pak seals around the wires. To avoid damage, do not use Tee pins in the front side of the connector where it plugs into another connector.

Use alligator clips and leads to attach the Tee pins to the DVOM. On analog sensors, unplug the connector and then attach either lead to either wire leading to the sensor, not to the ABS computer.

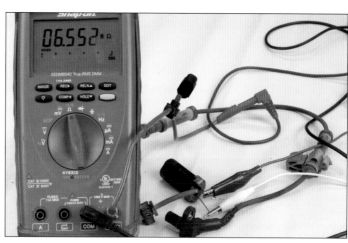

The DVOM should be set to measure ohms. The reading varies from vehicle to vehicle, but the resistance for an analog sensor is generally between 800 and 2,500 ohms. Temperature affects the reading. Some specs are given on a chart with temperature readings listed.

Put the meter in AC volts on a low range/scale (2–5 volts or so) and spin the wheel to see if AC voltage is generated. You should see more than 100 millivolts (0.1 volt) when spinning the wheel by hand. Some applications may generate 2 or 3 volts depending on how fast you spin the wheel by hand.

Analog Scope Testing

A digital storage oscilloscope (DSO) can also be used to test a WSS. It is the most effective method but not generally used in a home shop due to cost. A scope can display a "waveform" or the voltage signal using peaks and valleys. An AC waveform is known as a sine wave and displays the highest and lowest voltages recorded on a screen. It is a sort of visual voltmeter.

The advantage to using a scope is that each voltage pulse generated by the exciter ring teeth passing the sensor is visible and a broken tooth or low pattern from a weak sensor magnet can easily be seen. This is not

The DVOM needs to be set to the AC voltage scale on low range. Spin the wheel at about one revolution per second. You should see at least 100 millivolts as you spin the wheel. If you spin the wheel faster, you see about 2–3 volts AC. Some sensors put out as many as 90 volts AC on the highway but very low amperage.

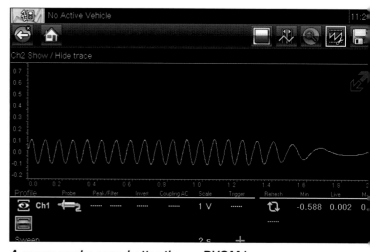

A scope works even better than a DVOM because you can "see" each voltage pulse and immediately know if a tooth is missing. You attach it in the same manner as the meter. This scope capture shows an AC voltage waveform as the wheel is spun by hand and slows to a stop. The highest output is 100 millivolts or about 1/10 volt AC.

possible with a DVOM since it averages the signal it sees and is not fast enough to record intermittent issues, or "drop outs," from a broken tooth.

DVOM Digital Sensor Testing

The process to test a digital sensor differs from analog sensor testing. A digital device is never tested for resistance (ohms) but can be tested for voltage. Instead of AC voltage, a digital sensor is tested using the DC volts scale on the meter. You do not unplug the WSS connector on vehicles with digital wheel speed sensors because they do not generate their own voltage but rather receive battery voltage from the EBCM and return a lower voltage pulsing signal as the wheel rotates.

Install a Tee pin in both of the two wires on the connector leading to the affected sensor and position them so that they do not touch each other. Turn on the ignition and use the meter in DC volts (20 volt scale).

Attach the black lead to a good ground and touch it to either of the Tee pins. One pin shows battery voltage and the other shows a voltage of about 0.8 or 1.65 volts.

Attach the red lead to the pin with the low voltage and turn the wheel very slowly. The signal should switch from about 0.5 to 1.5 volts. Some manufacturers may switch the battery voltage signal on and off as the wheel rotates. Be careful not to allow the Tee pins to touch. If they do, the EBCM

usually turns off the battery voltage to that wheel. To re-establish the voltage, simply turn the ignition off and back on.

Scope Testing a Digital Wheel Speed Sensor

You can attach the scope leads in the same manner as on the meter and set it up for DC square wave on a low-voltage scale. The switching shows a square wave pattern as the wheel is slowly rotated, allowing you

If the meter displays battery voltage, move the red lead to the other wire and turn the wheel very slowly. You see the voltage switch between about 0.8 and 1.65 VDC on a properly operating sensor. Be sure to turn it very slowly because it switches every time a tooth on the tone ring goes by. If you spin it too fast, they average and the reading is of no value to you.

Later-model vehicles use digital wheel speed sensors, which are supplied with battery voltage and switch a low-voltage DC pulse of about 0.8–1.65 DC. Place the DVOM on the DC scale and attach the black lead to a good ground. Leave the connector plugged in and back probe each wire with a Tee pin. Attach the red lead to either of the Tee pins. One reads battery voltage and the other shows approximately 0.8 or 1.65 VDC.

If you attach an oscilloscope and turn the wheel very slowly, you see a digital pattern on the screen. The voltage must be set low (2 or 5 VDC scale). This is the best way to see a missing or damaged tooth on the tone ring. Set the scope time base for 1 second.

to see each tone ring tooth as it goes by. A missing tooth is easy to find on a scope but not with a DVOM.

ABS-Related Systems

Many advanced systems, such as stability control and traction assist, use the ABS system to accomplish their goals. It makes sense that the ABS and the base brake system must both perform flawlessly for these other systems to work as designed.

Traction Assist

Traction assist systems are designed to reduce wheel spin and help a vehicle when it is in slippery conditions. The system can use engine management and/or brake interaction to pull a vehicle out of the mud or snow through the ABS system. If a wheel spins, the system generally reduces engine torque by reducing throttle opening or by disabling cylinders, adjusting ignition timing, or even upshifting the transmission. As a last resort, the system may apply the brakes to the spin-

ning wheel through the ABS system. Because of differential action in the drive axle, this causes torque to be applied to the other drive wheel, which likely has more traction and frees the vehicle from being stuck. Traction control has been referred to as "electronic positraction."

This system also functions when climbing a hill in slippery conditions such as snow. The system can transfer power from side to side to the wheel with the best traction. When a wheel begins to spin, the other stops and slightly sticks to the road. When the power comes back to that side, the system can gradually add power in an attempt to maintain traction. If the wheel starts to spin, the power shifts to the other side and the process continues until the vehicle "walks" up the hill.

Some vehicles display a message or lamp on the dashboard when the system is active. A blue "LOW TRAC" lamp or limited-traction message may appear when traction assist, ABS, or stability control systems are active. This is to advise the driver that there

are slippery conditions that he or she may not be aware of, such as black ice. Some German cars have a red or amber triangular lamp on the instrument panel that flashes when unsafe conditions cause any of these systems to engage. Some vehicles have a button on the dash that can disable traction control, but it resets to active when the ignition key is cycled.

Some vehicles have an "Active TRAC" lamp that illuminates when the system is responding to low-traction conditions. Most systems use the ABS sensors as an input to determine wheel spin by comparing non-drive-wheel speeds to drive-wheel speeds. This German-built vehicle displays a warning triangle anytime the vehicle is subjected to adverse conditions that enable a safety system.

Many vehicles have electronic traction assist. It uses the ABS system to monitor and control wheel spin by reducing torque or applying braking to a spinning wheel to force power to the wheel on the other side of the vehicle, which may have better traction.

The first step used by vehicle manufacturers to control wheel spin is usually to reduce torque by disabling fuel injectors, retarding spark, or reducing throttle opening. Some vehicles also upshift the transmission to reduce torque. If this does not get the vehicle out of the mud or snow, the brakes may be applied to the spinning wheel as a last resort.

Stability Control

Stability control systems also use the ABS system and the powertrain control module (PCM) to improve control around turns. If a vehicle enters a turn at a speed that could lead to loss of control, the system can reduce engine speed (RPM) to slow the vehicle and apply individual brakes at any wheel in an attempt to "steer" the vehicle and keep it on the road.

This system is effective and now is required on all vehicles weighing more than 10,000 pounds GVW sold in the United States beginning in 2012. Some manufacturers have offered this system for many years. Mercedes has had it available since 1995 and standard on all vehicles since 1998! It is totally automatic and research has shown it to have saved many lives. Of course, the system cannot stabilize a vehicle in all circumstances and is limited by conditions and traction levels.

The system uses a steering angle sensor, wheel speed sensors, and a vehicle speed sensor, but the heart of the system is a yaw sensor mounted in the center console of the vehicle that reports oversteer and understeer conditions to a control module, often the electronic brake and traction control module (EBTCM) or body control module (BCM). Some models use additional sensors, and future GPS interaction is planned that will slow the vehicle proactively when approaching a turn too rapidly. Today's systems are passive, meaning they react to conditions.

Oversteer is the most common condition that occurs when a vehicle enters a turn too rapidly. In racing this is called a "loose" condition. Engineers call it positive yaw rate. Regardless of the term used, the rear tires lose traction and the vehicle "steers" more than the steering wheel input. In other words, in a left turn the rear of the vehicle swings out to the right. The driver can sometimes save the skid by counter-steering to the right if the conditions allow, but often the vehicle slides sideways off the road into a ditch or tree. The stability control system reduces speed by limiting throttle and pulses the front or rear right-side wheel to counteract the oversteer condition.

Understeer can also occur when entering a turn too rapidly. In this case, the front wheels lose traction and the vehicle steers less than the steering wheel input. This is referred to as a "tight" condition in racing circles and negative yaw rate by engineers. On a left turn, the vehicle feels as if it is going straight, even though the steering wheel is turned to the left. The stability control system reduces throttle and applies pulsing left-side braking to attempt to steer the vehicle into the turn.

Professional race driver Ken Schrader once reported to me, "The main difference between understeer and oversteer is with understeer, you get to see what you are going to run into, but with oversteer you don't!"

Other Brake-Related Technologies

The base brake system that you are repairing must function properly for the ABS to work effectively. The ABS may also be used for more advanced vehicle systems, including electronic braking and as a component of the advanced driver assistance systems (ADAS). Without proper base brake and ABS operation, none of these systems can perform as intended. The following features all rely on the base brakes and ABS, so proper operation, service, adjustment, and parts quality is imperative.

Hill Holding

Some manual-shift vehicles use the ABS system to hold a vehicle on a hill so that it does not roll back when the brake is released and the clutch is engaged to move forward. This reduces the chance of rolling back into the vehicle behind you on a steep incline. The vehicle senses the incline and delays brake pressure release until the clutch is engaged and forward movement occurs. This is also found on automatic transmissions.

A yaw sensor mounted in the center of the vehicle can detect oversteer and understeer. The information gathered with input from other sensors allows the stability control system to use pulse braking to reduce extreme yaw rates and the potential of a vehicle crash.

Brake Descent Assist

Some newer models use hill descent assist so that the driver does not have to constantly apply the brakes when going downhill off road.

Highway Creep Control

Creep control is a system that automatically applies the brakes when the vehicle is in stop-and-go traffic. Each time the accelerator pedal is released, the brakes lightly apply so that the driver does not have to keep moving his or her foot from the brake to the accelerator.

Rainy Day Rotor Drying

Some vehicles can sense when it is raining and pulse the disc brakes intermittently, very lightly to keep the rotors dry. This is designed to provide more adequate braking on rainy days. Disc brakes perform much better than drum brakes in the rain due to squeegee action, but the rotor-drying feature adds another level of safety.

Pre-Safe

Some vehicles use on-board systems that precondition a vehicle for an accident. Sensors calculate the possibility and intensity of an impending crash and prepare the vehicle milliseconds before impact. Affected systems include airbags, seat position, seat belt pre-tensioners, sunroof and window closing, and may even use the radio. "Pink noise" is a sound generated by the sound system during a crash to reduce the impact of the noise made by airbag deployment on human hearing so that occupants are less tense.

Pre-Charge (Brake Assist)

Another feature that can reduce the chance of an accident or minimize damage and injury is brake pre-charging. When forward-facing sensors and deceleration rates indicate a possible accident, the system uses ABS pressure to increase the brake pressure to the wheels. Studies indicate that most drivers do not apply enough force fast enough when an accident is occurring.

ADAS Systems

Advanced Driver Assist Systems (ADAS) include many vehicle systems closely tied together. Some systems are relatively basic and others are advanced and may incorporate many vehicle systems and sensors to accomplish their goal. A trend in modern vehicles is to incorporate systems to achieve a higher level of driver comfort and safety.

Lane Change Warning

Some systems warn the driver during lane changing with another vehicle nearby. When the turn signal is on and the vehicle is steered toward another lane, a warning may be generated, either visually or audibly or both, and may become more intense as the collision possibility increases. Some vehicles may even vibrate the seat or steering wheel to get the attention of the driver.

Lane Change Assist

An enhancement to lane change warning is lane change assist. If

Many late-model vehicles have on-board radar sensors that send data to control modules that help steer, throttle, and brake the vehicle. Some of these monitor vehicles in the vicinity or watch the lines on the street. Such systems are known as ADAS or Advanced Driver Assist Systems.

A multitude of sensors are present behind the front fascia panel on this highly equipped ADAS vehicle. In the next few decades, these sensors will likely take complete control of the vehicle. Roadways mapped with the light detection and ranging (LIDAR) system will also be capable of controlling the vehicle with the assistance of the on-board sensors.

Some sensors require recalibration after wheel alignment or service including bodywork. Some are scan-tool driven and others are mechanical adjustments using targets similar to aligning headlights. In some cases, a large amount of flat ground is required in a shop environment with low light. Some are very time consuming.

Distance-based cruise control has been available for several years. The system can maintain a preset following distance between you and the vehicle in front of you. As the system has been refined, it now can stop the vehicle completely if needed, and in many cases, the cruise control does not have to be enabled. The main sensor for this system is usually mounted behind the grille.

This Mercedes has self-driving capabilities and is being used to test the automatic braking function. I was present for this test and the automatic braking feature performed flawlessly every time. It was surprising just how close the vehicle came to the simulated vehicle before full automatic braking was applied.

Some high-end vehicles and hybrids use a non-traditional brake system that does not use a common master cylinder. The brake pedal is simply a position sensor sending electrical signals to a module under the hood. The pressure is produced by a pump and stored in an HPA. When the brake pedal is applied, high-pressure fluid is sent to each wheel as needed by electronic solenoids in the module.

the driver does not make a correction after being warned, the system may take further action by steering the vehicle away from the possible collision. This is accomplished by using the electric assist power steering motor or pulsing individual brakes to steer the vehicle. Cameras, light detection and ranging (LIDAR), and ultrasonic and radar sensors are generally used as inputs to the system. Some of them require recalibration after wheel alignment, collision repair, or component or module replacement.

Distance-Based Cruise Control

For many years, manufacturers have offered distance-based cruise control (DBC). This system controls vehicle speed in the conventional manner and it adjusts throttle and applies the brakes to maintain a preset following distance behind another vehicle. On most applications with DBC, you can select the following distance you prefer.

A radar sensor in the grille or bumper opening sends a signal to the vehicle ahead, and brake and throttle control automatically main-

tain the preset following distance. If the driver ahead slows down, your vehicle also slows down. On later models, automatic braking may occur all the way to a dead stop.

Brake Warning and Automatic Brake Assist

Some vehicle manufacturers have taken distance-based cruise control to another level. The brakes can apply automatically with or without the cruise activated. In addition, an audible, visual, or physical warning may take place prior to automatic braking. The automatic braking

may be available for forward and/or reverse driving.

Electronic Braking

Many high-end and hybrid vehicles use electronic brake systems, which are a major departure from conventional braking systems. A brake pedal travel sensor is used to monitor driver input and the brakes are applied electronically. Some use a hydraulic pressure chamber similar to a miniature master cylinder with pressure transducers that measure pressure and convert it to electrical signals. This design produces

The mini-master cylinder contains two transducers and has a piston to simulate the familiar feel of a conventional brake system. When the brake is applied, the transducers convert pressure into electrical signals used by the modulator to apply the brakes. If there is a failure within the system, valves within the unit allow pressure from the mini-master to the front wheels for emergency braking.

a natural brake feel in the pedal for driver comfort.

The electrical signals are sent to a brake computer/modulator that calculates optimal braking for the present conditions and sends pressure to each wheel from a high-pressure pump/accumulator. There is no conventional master cylinder sending brake fluid to each wheel.

The computer/modulator contains a processor, high-pressure pump, accumulator, and hydraulic valves that actually apply the brakes instead of a conventional master cylinder. The advantage of this design is that brake fluid can be applied to any wheel at any pressure necessary for normal braking, ABS braking, proportioned braking during a panic stop (more pressure up front), or even side-to-side pressure variations during cornering.

During a panic stop, weight transfer to the front means that more braking is possible, but the rear is lighter, so less braking is applied. When cornering, the outboard wheels can handle more brake pressure due to weight transfer, so more braking at those wheels reduce stopping distance and improve safety.

The pressure chambers at the pedal sometimes contain solenoids that can open and route fluid to the front wheels in the event of system failure, but brake performance is limited since the fluid is not assisted. This is how the Mercedes Sensatronic system provides a failsafe if a problem occurs. On-board electronics provide detailed diagnosis using a scan tool. Available data display of various system pressures, component operation and trouble codes are used to determine the nature of the malfunction and repair it. In addition, multiple instrument panel lamps and warnings are displayed with audible warnings to advise the driver of a system problem.

For example, the accumulator may develop a leak over time and the computer can monitor how long it takes for the high-pressure pump to fill it when the system first initializes. The initialization takes place as you get close to the car before the key is in the ignition. As much as 2,000 psi can be present in the system before you open the door to get in.

If the time is too long, a code is set and a warning message appears

A failure within an electronic brake system can trigger multiple warnings, both visual and audible, so you are aware of the problem and can have it repaired. Extremely high pressure is present in the system, so all service procedures must be strictly followed before servicing it.

to "visit workshop." If the computer determines that operation would be dangerous, the warning becomes more direct and multiple lights and the audible warnings take place. If the vehicle is driven, a loud audible beep becomes more intense and closer together and every light on the dash illuminates.

On some modern vehicles, each wheel is controlled by a module based on conditions accessed from a variety of on-board sensors. These sensors include ABS wheel speed sensors, vehicle speed sensors, steering angle sensors, yaw rate sensors, lateral and longitudinal accelerometers (body roll and pitch), throttle position sensors, engine RPM sensors, brake pressure sensors, pedal travel sensors, radar sensors, light detection and ranging (LIDAR) mapping, and even cameras.

This is not a new concept and variations of this system have been used on some German vehicles for more than 10 years. As technology

A variety of codes can be set depending on the system malfunction. The codes are accessed with a scan tool and then used to determine the root cause of the problem using factory service procedures and a step-by-step approach known as a trouble tree. Most trouble trees start with testing circuits, power, and ground. Components are tested next. If they all prove out, the module is suspected. Some of these vehicles have extended warranties, so check with your dealer if you have problems.

Be Aware of Electronic Brake Self-Tests

Electronic brake systems can contain high-pressure brake fluid at all times and can also perform self-tests without warning; many wake up when the key fob is close to the vehicle and develop extremely high pressures in the system. Special precautions must be followed during service. Most electronic brake–equipped vehicles must be put into service mode with a scan tool prior to any service including a simple brake job/pad replacement.

If the system performed a self-test with the calipers off, the pistons could be exposed to high pressure, causing them to launch from the caliper, causing damage and injury. In addition, high-pressure fluid escaping can pierce through skin and enter the bloodstream, causing severe injury or death. Do not perform any service on a brake system that you are unfamiliar with prior to consulting the factory service information. This is especially true on vehicles equipped with ABS and electronic brake systems. Similar precautions relate to high-pressure diesel and gasoline direct-injection systems, and severe injury and death has occurred. This must not be taken lightly! Even a basic repair could require an advanced process. ∎

has progressed, sensors have been added and the systems have been incorporated with the ADAS. It is expected that more and more sensors will be added to the vehicles of the future especially when autonomous vehicles emerge. Sensors have been traditionally the main flaw because of their locations on the vehicle in past systems.

These systems interact with stability control, traction assist, distance-based cruise control, and various other systems on the vehicle. ADAS uses individual brake pulses from the electronic brake system for steering correction related to lane use and stability control in some cases. All of these systems rely on the base brake system that you are servicing when you do a simple brake job. It is critical to perform service correctly and use replacement parts that perform like the original equipment parts did to ensure the proper operation of these extremely sensitive systems.

Electronic Wedge Braking

Electronic wedge braking (EWB) is an experimental system that is being pioneered in Europe by the Siemens Corporation. It is a disc brake system using electricity instead of hydraulics to apply the calipers. It uses a traditional sliding caliper, but that is where the similarity ends.

Instead of a hydraulically actuated piston extending to apply the inboard pad, two small motors push a plate back and forth, which has a series of "speed bumps" on it. The inboard pad also has these bumps between the bumps on the plate when the brakes are not applied. When braking is required, one motor slides the plate, which causes the bumps on the plate to push the bumps on the pad away and into the spinning rotor. The spinning action of the rotor causes the pad to attempt to move with it, and this action self-energizes the pad by a wedging effect. In other words, the pad touching the spinning rotor makes it "climb" up the bumps and wedge itself into the rotor, stopping the vehicle. The motors don't have to be extremely powerful since the friction contact with the rotor self-energizes the pad. When braking is no longer

Many newer brake systems, such as on this Prius, use stored high pressure to apply the brakes. This pressure can be built up even before the key is in the vehicle. A high-pressure pump charges an HPA with thousands of pounds of brake fluid pressure. A scan tool may be required to disable the system prior to servicing. Follow all manufacturer procedures.

Most electronic brake systems such as on this Lexus must be disabled during a brake job so that the high pressure does not cause injury to the technician. If the system is left active and it performs a self-test during a brake job, a caliper piston could be expelled causing serious injury. Consult service information for the vehicle you are working on before beginning any repairs.

needed, the other motor pushes the plate back and the brakes release.

EWB can be compared to the duo-servo drum brake system, which also uses self-energizing to increase brake force. The spinning drum makes the shoe wedge itself against the friction surface to stop the vehicle. Many new concepts are variations of old concepts.

Regen Braking

Regen (regenerative) braking is used on many hybrid and battery-powered vehicles. It is a function of the electric motor/generator that is used to propel the vehicle. The vehicle has conventional brakes with rotors and pads, but they are generally smaller because the vehicle also has regen brakes.

When the brake pedal is applied, the motor/generator becomes a generator, which does two things: It charges the main drive battery by using the deceleration of the vehicle to turn the generator shaft, and it provides braking for the vehicle. In other words, the conventional brake is only needed when the vehicle approaches a dead stop or in panic situations. The brakes could conceivably last the life of the vehicle if the driver is not overly aggressive.

Some driving situations, such as in the mountains, need more braking. When descending a mountain road, the regen system may fully charge the battery and then shut down. At that time, the base brakes have to kick in and stop the vehicle, which could put an immense strain on them and cause them to wear out rapidly due to their smaller size.

Most hybrids have a solution for this by providing engine braking during these conditions. An example is the Toyota Prius, which has a gear-

The Toyota Prius has been around for many years and is one of the first vehicles to use regenerative braking. The system uses the drive motor as a generator during stopping through magnetism. This action recharges the on-board battery and gives adequate braking in most conditions. The vehicle has a disc brake system for emergency stopping and adverse conditions, but the regen braking does most of the work during normal driving.

shift position known as the "B" mode. For driving on level roads, the transmission shifter is placed in the normal "D" position, but in the mountains, the "B" mode (for engine braking) should be selected. This mode causes the engine to assist in slowing the vehicle during hill descent to protect the conventional brake system from damage. Many Prius owners are unaware of this requirement.

The Importance of Communication

Within the next few decades, we will likely see Level 5 autonomy, including self-driving vehicles with no steering wheel, throttle, or brake pedal. There will still be brakes that need to be serviced, whether they are actuated by a driver or not.

Vehicle manufacturers are beginning to incorporate more advanced communications between vehicles, their surroundings, and

This is a Tesla battery. It mounts under the vehicle and is partially charged by regen braking. Some newer models are even using suspension movement to supply electricity to recharge the drive battery. You can expect this method of vehicle propulsion to increase significantly in the future.

even with pedestrians through their cellphones. Like it or not, people don't always pay attention while they are driving or even walking. Electronics can be our friend as evidenced by the tremendous advancements in the cars we drive. But they can also be our enemy when we are distracted.

Communication Increasing

To help with this problem are vehicle-to-infrastructure (V2I), vehicle-to-vehicle (V2V), and vehicle-to-everything (V2E) communication. Brakes and vehicle control will be an integral part of this.

V2I

V2I communication allows a vehicle to connect with its stationary surroundings, such as stoplights, road signs (speed limits that are also available through on-board GPS), and government regulations for that state. This could include dash messages about trailer towing, low bridges ahead, motorcycle helmet laws, speed limits, fog conditions, accidents ahead; the list could go on and on.

Using these communications, all vehicles can be stopped at intersections when an emergency vehicle approaches because the infrastructure can sense the vehicle coming into the intersection and turn all stoplights to red. This could also occur if someone is approaching the intersection at high speed and the light is red. The system can warn vehicles approaching the intersection with a message on their dash or even apply brakes automatically to their vehicles so that they are not hit by the vehicle running the light.

When traveling on a road with multiple stoplights, the speed of a vehicle can be controlled for timing so that no red lights are encountered. The promise of this system could improve the flow of traffic to avoid starts and stops and reduce rear-end collisions. Conditions such as snow and ice could be calculated into the equation so that vehicles are traveling at the maximum speed for the conditions. Vehicles approaching an accident in the fog at highway speeds could be stopped before a 25-car pileup occurs, reducing countless injuries and property damage.

Modern vehicles have current technology that would allow external control of throttle, braking, and even steering since many vehicles have electric assist power steering and even drive-by-wire technology. This would allow law enforcement to virtually eliminate high-speed chases.

With GPS interaction, there may come a day when vehicles are not able to exceed the speed limit. Although controversial, the intent is to reduce traffic fatalities from speeding. A benefit to this control system is reducing accidents on curves. As a vehicle with the system approaches a curve too fast, the GPS anticipates the curve ahead and slows the vehicle prior to the curve. Currently, stability control actively uses engine control and selective braking to help a speeding vehicle through the curve, but that is after the mistake has been made (reactive).

The future system would be proactive, preventing the mistake by slowing the vehicle before the curve. This is not a big stretch because an inexpensive aftermarket GPS knows where you are and what the speed limit is and many ADAS cameras can already recognize road signs.

LIDAR can map roads in 360 degrees and is going to be mainstream when autonomous vehicles appear.

Cadillac is already using LIDAR as part of its Super Cruise self-driving system. It is the main input during self-driving with the aid of sensors and cameras.

In operation, the Cadillac Super Cruise system uses an illuminated strip at the top of the steering wheel with system status. A green light strip means that it is self-driving. It can turn red or blue if other conditions exist. Only roads that have been previously mapped by LIDAR can allow self-driving. The car watches your eyes and if you are distracted for too long, it forces you to grab the steering wheel. If you ignore it, it produces several warnings, both visually and audibly and then begins to slow and eventually stop the vehicle with the emergency flashers on. It uses sensors and cameras in addition to the LIDAR mapping.

Cadillac Super Cruise is one of the first systems to allow a vehicle to drive itself. It uses nationwide LIDAR mapping and a multitude of sensors and cameras to accomplish this task. The driver is monitored and can be summoned to take over the controls if the system detects driver inattention or is confused by poor driving conditions or detours. Autonomous operation is not legal in some areas.

Mercedes offers a vehicle with partial self-driving capabilities using on-board sensors exclusively. It can also park itself in any parking spot.

The Super Cruise system monitors the driver and asks him or her to take over control in certain situations. If the driver does not respond to increasingly louder and more aggressive prompts, the vehicle can slow and stop on its own and actuate the emergency flashers. It may also be able to summon help through the ONSTAR system in the future if the driver is unresponsive.

We may see steering wheels disappear, but brakes will still need to be serviced.

V2V

V2V communications can report icy conditions, accidents, or high-traffic areas to other vehicles in the area so that they can avoid or be prepared for it. For example, some current vehicles can communicate with other vehicles of the same brand when one has an ABS stop. GPS coordinates are broadcast and dash warnings can alert other vehicles in the area to that slippery spot. The hope is that all vehicles could communicate with each other in the future.

Rear-facing radar systems already in place can warn you of an impending rear-end collision and prepare the vehicle for impact, slightly moving it forward. Some vehicles currently have technology that lifts one side of a vehicle prior to a side impact. Others have explosive charges and seat airbags to tilt the seat and move the passengers' heads inboard away from the window prior to an unavoidable side impact.

V2E

V2E communications allow the vehicle to communicate with more of its surroundings, even cell phones. If a pedestrian is not paying attention and starts to step off a curb, vehicles approaching could have warnings or automatic braking applied. The pedestrian's cell phone may emit a high-pitched warning to stop him or her from stepping off the curb if vehicles are present.

Final Thoughts

Although there will be challenges and skeptics will cling to the old-school vehicles, there is no argument that there are many exciting technologies right around the corner. Whether your preference is to drive a new Cadillac with Super Cruise or a 1970 Chevelle, your brakes need to perform as intended and be serviced to continue to do so.

You should now have the confidence to service modern brake systems. You also need to have access to service information and have the right tools. Never stop learning. Practice your skills and take pleasure in your accomplishments. Study hard, but take a *brake* now and then!

This 1970 Chevelle uses friction to stop just as a brand-new Cadillac with Super Cruise does. If you can fix one, you can fix the other, so don't be intimidated by either extreme. All you need is knowledge, the right tools, and confidence. Factory service information will be increasingly important in the future.

DISC AND DRUM COMPLETE BRAKE JOB

Front Disc Brake Replacement

This is the project vehicle. It has front disc brakes, rear drum brakes, and ABS. It is from the Midwest in the snow belt and has normal rust for that region.

Be sure to follow recommended safety practices before you begin, including the use of safety glasses, disposable rubber gloves, and ear protection. Rotary equipment can shed debris that can enter your eyes or skin, so use caution. Have a fire extinguisher on hand, just in case, and plenty of shop towels or paper towels. Check all technical service bulletins (TSBs) and service procedures to see if any precautions must be followed prior to the brake job. Some high-end and hybrid vehicles require that the electronic brake system is shut down prior to any brake system service.

Be sure to use the proper lubricants and thread sealer when required. Never use petroleum-based lubricants on rubber or synthetic brake components. Do not confuse silicone lubricant with silicone sealer. Using too much lubricant can cause caliper slides to hydrolock.

Many late-model vehicles have electronic brake systems. Some of them require that the system be placed in service mode before working on the system. This is done with a scan tool, but there are some "work arounds" to accomplish it on some applications. This step is important because high-pressure fluid in the system can cause severe injury. This particular vehicle did not require this step.

Preparing the Vehicle

1 The first step is to raise the hood and place fender covers over the painted surfaces. Then wipe away dirt and dust from around the master cylinder reservoir lid and carefully remove it. Using a turkey baster or vacuum bleeder, draw out all of the old brake fluid and place it in a container for proper disposal.

2 Refer to the lid of the master cylinder for the proper DOT brake fluid rating. Most vehicles use DOT 3 or DOT 4 brake fluid. Fill the master cylinder to the MAX line, but do not overfill. Install the reservoir lid and wipe away any spilled brake fluid. Caution: Brake fluid is very harmful to painted surfaces.

3 Slightly loosen the lug nuts or bolts on the first front wheel, but do not loosen them to the point that they are free. If you are using an impact wrench to remove the fasteners, this step is not necessary. Lift and support the vehicle first.

4 Place the gear selector in Park for automatic transmission vehicles, or in First or Reverse gear for manual shift vehicles, and apply the parking brake. Place wheel chocks at the front and rear of both rear wheels.

5 Place a floor jack with adequate capacity rating in the appropriate position under the jacking point for the vehicle. Consult service information or the American Lift Institute (ALI) guide and raise the vehicle high enough to install a jack stand on both sides. On some applications you may have to raise one side at a time.

6 Let the weight of the vehicle down on the jack stands so that the floor jack is no longer supporting the weight of the vehicle. Be sure that the jack stand positions are safe before you proceed.

Front Disc Brake Disassembly and Inspection

1 Remove the previously loosened wheel fasteners and mark the wheel position to one stud, so you can index the wheel to the same position when reinstalling the wheel after the brake job. Set the wheel safely aside.

2 Take a photo of the brake system before disassembly. Pay particular attention to the position and routing of the brake hose so that it is not twisted or misrouted during reassembly.

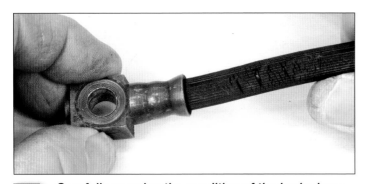

4 If the brake hose requires replacement, you need to loosen the banjo bolt from the caliper and the fitting where it attaches to the brake line. When loosening the banjo bolt, brake fluid will escape, so place a drain pan underneath.

3 Carefully examine the condition of the brake hose, especially near the crimped ends that fasten the hose to the fittings on each end. Any cracks you find means that the hose should be replaced.

5 A common tire valve stem does a good job of temporarily sealing the leak after banjo bolt removal, but don't leave it in too long because the rubber will swell and make it difficult to remove.

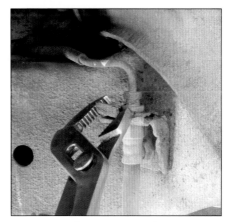

6 Use flare nut wrenches to remove the steel line from the hose fitting. A spring clip holds the hose to a bracket on the inner fenderwell. It can be removed with slip-joint pliers. A new one comes with the new hose.

Most lines have a special hex nut flat that can only be installed in one position so that the hose is correctly positioned to allow slack during steering.

Front Disc Brake Disassembly and Inspection *(Continued)*

7 *It is important to make sure that the bleeder screw can be loosened so that you can bleed the brakes after you have completed the brake job. Using the appropriate wrench, loosen the bleeder and then retighten it to avoid brake fluid loss. Most bleeders require a 10-mm wrench; some require an 8-mm wrench. It is best to use a six-point socket or box end so that the flats do not round off. If the bleeder is seized, refer to chapter 3: Disc Brake System for additional information.*

8 *Remove the fasteners that attach the caliper to the caliper bracket or steering knuckle. Most models use a common bolt or a Torx bolt that threads into a slide where the caliper rides. The slide may need to be held in place with a wrench to allow removal of the fastener.*

9 *Remove the caliper from the rotor by gently prying under the caliper with a flat-blade screwdriver. Be careful not to allow the brake pads to fall from the caliper as you pull it off the rotor.*

10 *To avoid hose damage, do not allow the caliper to hang by the brake hose. Using an S-shaped hook, rubber strap, or heavy wire, hang the caliper securely from a solid component such as the coil spring or from a bracket so that no weight is on the hose.*

11 *With the brake caliper securely supported, you can remove the brake pads from the caliper or bracket. Some brake pads use clips and the pad must be pried away from the caliper to allow removal. Many inboard pads have three spring clips that hold the pad inside the bore of the caliper piston. In most cases, you can easily pull the brake pad from the caliper piston.*

12 *Examine the caliper slides and pins to make sure that they move freely. Be certain that the caliper pistons and dust seals are not damaged or worn excessively where the pads make contact with it. Inspect for brake fluid leakage around the piston dust seal. If any of these issues are present, the caliper should be replaced at this time.*

13 *Some vehicles use a separate caliper bracket between the caliper and the knuckle. It must be removed to allow rotor removal. Two bolts are used that are usually very tight due to high torque and thread-locking compound. Note: Some newer vehicles have bolts that cannot be reused. Check the factory service information for further details.*

Front Disc Brake Disassembly and Inspection *(Continued)*

14 *A micrometer should be used to measure the remaining rotor thickness. Compare your readings to factory service information or the minimum-thickness spec cast into the rotor. If it is below specifications, it must be replaced. If the rotor requires machining, it must have enough material left to be above specifications after machining. Inspect the rotor for deep grooves, hard spots, and surface condition. Also check for thickness variation and excessive rotor runout if you want to reuse the rotor, especially if the vehicle had a brake pulsation when stopping. Refer to chapter 3 for more details.*

15 *To check for excessive rotor runout, a dial indicator can be used. Reinstall the lug nuts to hold the rotor against the hub flange. Most manufacturers do not allow more than about 0.004 inch of runout. If the rotor is beyond specification but still within thickness tolerance, it can be machined or replaced. This is a personal preference, but it's usually best to stick with a known supplier if you choose to replace the rotor. Rotors should be replaced in pairs to avoid problems such as a brake pull to one side.*

16 *If you plan to reuse the rotor, mark one stud position to the rotor so that it can be reinstalled in the same position. This prevents increased runout between the two components.*

17 *Remove the rotor and place it face up. Avoid touching the friction surfaces.*

Preparation for Reassembly

1 Clean the contact surfaces on the rotor, hub, and backside of the wheel with a rotary buffer tool. This reduces the possibility of inducing runout and brake pulsation. Also, any rust left behind can be crushed after reassembly and lead to a loose wheel as the vehicle is driven.

3 A special tool is also available for retracting the caliper piston. It can sometimes be borrowed from your local parts store or is a good investment if you plan to do brake jobs regularly in the future.

2 If the caliper is to be reused, push the piston back into its bore in the caliper with a clamp or special tool. You can use one of the old brake pads and a common C-clamp for this purpose, but you need to open the bleeder first so that the old fluid can escape instead of flowing back through the ABS unit and into the master cylinder. Place a pan under the caliper and keep the bleeder at the top to avoid air entering the system.

4 Clean and inspect the caliper slides, pins, and associated hardware. If they are worn or damaged, the pins and rubber components are available separately. If the caliper slides cannot be freed or the caliper is damaged or worn, replacement is necessary.

5 Lube the caliper slides and pins with the proper disc brake lubricant. Do not use anti-seize or any petroleum-based lubricant such as chassis or wheel bearing grease on rubber components because they will swell and likely seize. If a rubber bushing is over greased, it can hydrolock and cause one pad to drag on the rotor.

Front Disc Brake Reassembly

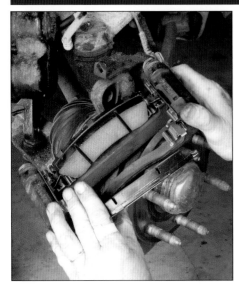

1 The old caliper hardware may be damaged by heat or wear and should be replaced with new hardware to reduce the possibility of brake noise. In many cases, new hardware is supplied with the replacement brake pads. Be sure that it fits properly and you put the correct clips in the right places. You often find subtle differences between inboard and outboard hardware and between left and right sides.

2 Lube the contact surfaces and install the new pads in the caliper after the new hardware and shims have been attached. Some pad shims are preinstalled and some must be installed prior to installation in the caliper. Most applications have inboard and outboard pads. Many have a mechanical wear indicator that must be put in the same place as the factory pad.

3 If the rotor requires machining or replacement, now is the time. Most auto parts stores can measure the rotor thickness to determine if they are within specifications and are able to be machined. If they are not, new rotors must be purchased. Make sure that the rotors have a smooth surface before installing them or extra pedal force will be required to stop.

4 Be sure to wash the machined rotor with hot water and soap to remove any contamination on the friction surface that could end up in the pads and cause noise and performance problems. Do not handle the friction surfaces.

5 New rotors are often shipped in plastic bags and coated with oil or a waxy coating to reduce rust formation during shipment from overseas. This needs to be removed prior to installation. Some German vehicle manufacturers put a gray primer-like coating on the rotor friction surface, which should not be removed prior to installation.

6 Install the new or machined rotor on the previously cleaned hub flange and install two lug nuts finger tight. This makes it easier to install the caliper because the rotor is at the proper angle. Some vehicle manufacturers do not require rotor machining or replacement during pad replacement. If you reuse your rotors "as is" be sure that they are within all vehicle specifications.

Front Disc Brake Reassembly *(Continued)*

7 If a caliper bracket is used, install the pads in the bracket against the new properly lubed hardware and then install the bracket. Be sure to apply thread locker to the attachment bolts. Some models require bolt replacement because they are torque-to-yield versions.

9 If the pads mount in the caliper instead of the caliper bracket, install them now and install the caliper over the rotor, making sure that the brake pads remain in their proper position. Be sure that the brake hose is properly positioned. Refer to the photo you took earlier to ensure that you have everything in the proper position. A twisted brake hose can break when turning the vehicle and cause a safety concern.

8 Torque both caliper bracket bolts to the factory specification with thread-locking compound on the threads. Be sure that no brake lubricant gets on the rotor surface and make sure that the pad hardware does not contact the rotor. This is also a good time to make sure that the splash shield on the inside of the rotor is not touching the rotor. If it is, pry it away from the rotor. This is a common source of noise after suspension or brake work has been done on a vehicle at a repair shop.

11 Move your tools to the front wheel on the other side of the vehicle and repeat the above steps on the other front brake.

10 Position the caliper so that the bolt holes line up with those in the steering knuckle or caliper bracket. Install and torque the caliper bolts to specification. If a new hose or caliper was installed, be sure to use new copper washers and torque the banjo bolt to manufacturer's specifications. Overtorquing results in bolt breakage and undertorquing results in a leak.

Brake Bleeding and Leak Testing

1 It is important to bleed the brakes so that new brake fluid can fill the system and all air is removed from the hydraulic system. Refer to Chapter 6: Hydraulic Brake System for details on bleeding.

2 After bleeding, fill the master cylinder reservoir to the MAX line. Don't overfill the reservoir or the brakes can drag or lock on when the fluid expands during brake operation.

3 It is important to pump up the brake pedal and check pedal feel. Have an assistant look for leaks at the front wheels while you apply high pedal force. Some technicians start the engine during the leak test. One of the main causes of accidents in an automotive shop is for someone to back out before they pumped up the brakes after a brake job.

4 Install the wheel and tire assemblies and torque them to specifications. Have an assistant hold the brake pedal or lower the vehicle until the tire just contacts the road and then use a torque wrench to tighten each lug nut in a star pattern to manufacturer's specifications. Torque them again in a circle to make sure that you did not miss any lugs.

Hoisting the Vehicle and Rear Wheel Brake Shoe Replacement

1 Before you move to the rear, place the wheel chocks on each side of both front wheels. Position a floor jack in a safe position and raise the vehicle enough so that the tires are off the ground and a jack stand can be placed under the frame or unibody in the correct position on both sides of the vehicle. On some applications you may have to raise one side at a time.

2 Lower the jack so that the weight rests on the jack stand. The jack stand should not be placed under the vehicle as a "back up" to the floor jack because jack stands are not rated for shock loading (vehicle weight falls onto the jack stand if the floor jack fails).

3 Remove the lug nuts and put them in a safe place. If the wheel is seized to the drum or hub, put a couple of lug nuts back on a few threads and hit the edge of the wheel with a rubber hammer. (Another option is to snug all the lug nuts and let the vehicle down and then pull forward and reverse to allow the vehicle weight to free the wheel.)

Rear Brake Disassembly

1 Mark the position of the brake drum to one stud and remove the drum.

2 If the vehicle has Tinnerman nuts securing the drums, it is likely that the vehicle has never had a rear brake job. Remove the Tinnerman nuts with side cutters and discard them. Some applications use screws, which must also be removed prior to removing the drum and reinstalled afterward.

3 Remove the brake drum. It may be necessary to tap it to free the rust bond around the center pilot hole or axle flange. If the drum is difficult to remove additional information can be found in Chapter 4: Drum Brake System.

4 Before you begin service, clean away the brake dust with brake cleaner spray and a drain pan. In a service facility, a special portable sink called a "bird bath" is used for this purpose. This is the preferred method but may not practical for home use. Brake dust often contains harmful substances. Be careful not to inhale any dust.

Rear Brake Disassembly (Continued)

5 Snap a photo of the drum brake components prior to removal so that you can get them back together correctly during reassembly. You can also leave the other side together to use as a point of reference.

6 Because drum brake work is dirtier than disc brake work, some people prefer to wear disposable gloves during the process. These are available in boxes of 100 and are relatively inexpensive and can be purchased at most auto parts stores.

7 Loosen the bleeder on the wheel cylinder to make sure that you can bleed the system after service. If you plan to replace the wheel cylinder, this step is not necessary. Retighten the bleeder so that you don't lose fluid from the system prior to proceeding with the brake job.

8 This particular truck uses a single-loop spring, which serves as both hold-down and return springs. A special tool is available to remove and install this spring, which makes the job much easier, but the brakes can be serviced without the tool.

9 Using a screwdriver, pry one end of the loop spring away from the brake shoe. There will be some tension on this spring, so use caution. It is easier to begin with the shoe that does not have the parking brake lever attached to it.

10 Pry the other side of the loop spring away from the other shoe. The shoes and the spring are loose on the backing plate but cannot be removed until the adjuster mechanism is removed.

Rear Brake Disassembly (Continued)

11 Use needle-nosed pliers to remove the adjuster lever tension spring. Pay attention to how it was installed so that you can reassemble it correctly. If this spring is improperly installed, the brakes do not self-adjust as they wear and the result is a low brake pedal.

12 The adjuster lever must be in good condition and able to turn the star wheel teeth when contact is made. If it is worn or bent, replacement is necessary. This part has a left- and right-side version as does most adjuster hardware. Sometimes it is stamped with an "L" or an "R" to differentiate them.

13 Before removing the star wheel adjuster assembly, take a good look at how it is installed between the shoes so that you can reinstall it properly.
Installing it backward or with the wrong fork in the shoe affects proper auto adjustment and the part could fall into the drum, causing damage.

14 After the loop spring and adjuster have been disconnected from the shoe, it should come out from under the loop spring without much effort. Inspect the shoe for uneven wear or contamination. If you find brake fluid or 90W gear oil, the source must be repaired prior to finishing the brake work.

15 Remove the brake shoe from under the loop spring with the parking brake lever attached to it. After it is away from the backing plate, the cable can be disconnected from the lever. For this application, the parking brake lever comes attached to the new shoe.

Rear Brake Disassembly (Continued)

16 *After you remove the shoes from under the loop spring, you can remove the spring from the backing plate. The spring is under a hook at the bottom in the center. Lift it upward to remove it.*

17 *The first step in wheel cylinder replacement is to loosen the brake line nut at the wheel cylinder. A flare nut wrench is preferred to reduce the chance of rounding off the nut. Place a pan under the area and remove the line from the wheel cylinder.*

Rear Brake Cleaning and Reassembly

1 *The wheel cylinder is attached to the backing plate with two 10-mm bolts or a spring clip (on GM applications). Remove the attachments and the wheel cylinder should come free of the backing plate. In some cases, rust may be holding the wheel cylinder. A large screwdriver can be used to pry the wheel cylinder away from the backing plate. Replacement is the reverse of removal. It is helpful to start the line prior to attaching the wheel cylinder to the backing plate to avoid stripping the line threads. After installation, be sure to torque the bolts and the brake line.*

2 *The backing must be thoroughly cleaned and dried before reassembly. A stiff-bristle brush and some brake cleaner spray will do a pretty good job of cleaning this area.*

Rear Brake Cleaning and Reassembly (Continued)

3 Each brake shoe is supported by three raised areas on the backing plate known as shoe support pads. Inspect them for grooves that can cause the shoes to make a popping sound when applied or released. If no grooves are found, lubricate them with the appropriate grease prior to shoe installation.

4 The brake drum should be smooth and free of large cracks, grooves, or hot spots. If you are replacing the drum you need to know the diameter to make sure that the parts store sells you the right parts. Many truck applications have several drum diameters as options.

5 Another helpful piece of information you can provide to the parts store to help you purchase the correct parts is the VIN of the vehicle, especially the last eight digits. This helps the counterperson look up the parts.

6 To avoid leaving greasy fingerprints on the new brake shoes, cover them with masking tape. After the shoes are completely installed, remove the tape immediately before installing the brake drum. Any time shoes are found to be contaminated with grease or brake fluid, they should be replaced.

7 Push the cable into the lever retainer until it snaps into place. You may have to tension the spring and hold it with some needle-nosed pliers through the coils. Carefully examine it to make sure it is fully engaged.

8 Attach the loop spring in the center retainer claw under the bearing hub. After applying a thin layer of lubricant to the shoe support pads on the backing plate, install the front brake shoe onto the backing plate. The special tool provides easier installation of the loop spring, but this can usually be accomplished with a common large screwdriver. Pry the loop spring into the correct hole in the shoe.

9 The rear shoe is installed in the same manner as the front shoe. Be sure to apply a thin layer of lubricant to the shoe support pads on the backing plate prior to the installation of the shoe. Pry the loop spring into the correct hole in the shoe.

Rear Brake Cleaning and Reassembly *(Continued)*

10 *After installation, be sure that the shoes are positioned in the wheel cylinder pistons properly and also in the lower anchor plate. With a hammer handle, push on the loop spring on both sides to make sure that the ends are fully engaged.*

11 *Install the new star wheel in the same position as the old one. Refer to your phone photo if necessary. Lube the threads and the end cap prior to installation.*

12 *Install the adjuster lever and spring. Be sure that the end of the lever properly contacts the teeth on the star wheel. If the alignment is not correct, the brake cannot adjust as the shoes wear and this results in a low brake pedal.*

13 *Before installing the brake drum, remove and discard the protective tape from the shoe friction surfaces. The tape keeps contamination off the new friction surface. Check the drum surface and compare the diameter to specs.*

14 *If needed, machine or replace the drum. It is a good idea to replace drums or rotors in pairs to reduce the possibility of a brake pull after the job. A difference in surface finish or material from side to side can result in a pull.*

15 *If the drum was machined or replaced, it is a good idea to thoroughly clean the drum with hot water, soap, and a bristle brush before installation. Some new drums are coated with a wax or oil-based protectant and may need to be sprayed with brake cleaner first.*

Rear Brake Cleaning and Reassembly *(Continued)*

16 *Adjust the star wheel so that the drum slides on with a little resistance but is still able to turn with a small amount of drag. This is known as a "slip fit." If there is too much of a gap between the shoes and drum, the brake pedal is low when applied. If there is too little of a gap, the brakes drag and cause damage to the new shoes. Final adjustment can be made after the drums are on and the vehicle has been bled. Move to the other side of the vehicle and repeat the process.*

17 *Slide the drum on and install two lug nuts or the tapered screws (if equipped) to hold it in position temporarily.*

18 *If the wheel cylinders were replaced, they must be properly bled to remove all of the air from the hydraulic system. Have an assistant press down on the brake about halfway and open the bleeder with a pan underneath. Close the bleeder and release the pedal. Reapply the pedal and repeat the process until clean fluid flows from the bleeders with no air bubbles. Check for leaks and top off the master cylinder to the max line.*

19 *Install the wheel and tire assemblies and torque them to specifications. Have an assistant hold the brake pedal or lower the vehicle until the tire just contacts the road and then use a torque wrench to tighten each lug nut in a star pattern to manufacturer's specifications. Then torque them again in a circle to make sure that you did not miss any lugs.*

20 *Test drive the vehicle and burnish in the new friction material according to manufacturer's guidelines. This is usually accomplished by 20-30 light pedal applications from 30 mph to a stop or 50- to 30-mph slowdowns with a 30-second cool-down period between them. Avoid panic stops. This is important because the new friction and rotor or drum surfaces have not yet "worn in" to each other. In time, the two will take on a mirror-like finish, which provides the best surface contact and optimal braking. Back up the vehicle and apply the brakes and the parking brakes. This further adjusts the rear brake shoes so that proper adjustment is achieved and the brake pedal is at the proper height. Check the master cylinder fluid level one last time and fill to the max line.*